CREATIVE *Awakenings*

Envisioning the Life of Your Dreams Through Art

Sheri Gaynor

NORTH LIGHT BOOKS
Cincinnati, Ohio

www.mycraftivity.com

13 12 11 10 09   5 4 3

Distributed in Canada by Fraser Direct
100 Armstrong Avenue
Georgetown, ON, Canada L7G 5S4
Tel: (905) 877-4411

Distributed in the U.K. and Europe by David & Charles
Brunel House, Newton Abbot, Devon, TQ12 4PU, England
Tel: (+44) 1626 323200, Fax: (+44) 1626 323319
E-mail: postmaster@davidandcharles.co.uk

Distributed in Australia by Capricorn Link
P.O. Box 704, S. Windsor, NSW 2756 Australia
Tel: (02) 4577-3555

Library of Congress Cataloging-in-Publication Data

Gaynor, Sheri,
  Creative awakenings: Envisioning the Life of Your Dreams Through Art / Sheri Gaynor.
     p. cm.
  Includes index.
  ISBN-13: 978-1-60061-115-5 (pbk. : alk. paper)
  1. Handicraft. 2. Handicraft--Blogs. I. Title.
  TT157.G38 2009
  615.8'5156--dc22

  2008032302

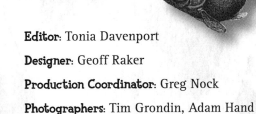

Editor: Tonia Davenport

Designer: Geoff Raker

Production Coordinator: Greg Nock

Photographers: Tim Grondin, Adam Hand

fw
media
www.fwmedia.com

My Heartfelt Dedication

For my parents Marilyn Itkin Gaynor and Michael Gaynor, for always reminding me I could be "whatever I wanted to be when I grew up." To my brother, Adam Gaynor, whose pursuit of the impossible taught me in the most extraordinary of ways, "When you believe, dreams do come true."

For my husband, Andrew Chase Putnam, who bestowed his love of the mountains and rivers on this city girl. I believe in my heart that the seeds of this book began with you. You have been my greatest teacher in being my authentic self and becoming a Feisty Female. "Trust your gut!" are words that continue to inspire me.

For maternal and paternal grandparents, entrepreneurs all, and the ultimate dreamers. You took the road less traveled and stepped into your dreams. My grandfather, Abe Itkin, took many of the vintage photographs you see in this book. I wish my grandparents were alive to see this, but somehow I have a sense they know.

In Memoriam: A Truly Feisty Female,
Anne Putnam Mallinson
1939-2008

Dedicated to the ultimate Feisty Female Beloved Aunt Annie

Chase...Margie...Annie...Murray

With So Much Gratitude and Love

A big thank-you to the following. My editor, Tonia Davenport, for seeing the possibilities, and believing the timing was right. To my team at North Light Books, your creative vision is extraordinary! A mountain of gratitude to the phenomenal group of artists who contributed to this book. Thank you for believing in me and trusting the process.

To the Putnam clan, I am in awe of the creative energy that lives within each one of you. To the Marsh women, thank you for the years of love and support. To all my women friends, who are too great in numbers to name on this page, I pray you know who you are. I celebrate the years we have spent together traveling this rich and rewarding road of life.

To Cindy Dunn, Laura Kirk and Beth Zukowski, for standing by my side every step of this adventure. Your forthright honesty and brilliant words of wisdom were invaluable during the writing of this book. To my SWIRL Sisters: You are an inspiration to me, my lifeline to laughter, good food and—oh yes—a bit of writing too! It's my turn to cheer you

on from the sidelines. To Dream Riders: Your dreams are as sacred as my own. An extra special hug to Barbe C. for the weekend retreat at your yurt, and to Toni Grenko and Linda Drake for your constant love and sisterhood! To Carol Lloyd who gave me wings to fly all those years ago. Your generosity is not forgotten and is simply extraordinary!

To my clients and students who have taught me so much. Without you this book may never have been born. Thank you for co-creating with me—I am honored and blessed to have been witness to your many journeys.

To my beloved, free-spirited creative community at the base of Mount Sopris. This is a place where we make our dreams happen. I am grateful every day to be in our amazing community. Keep on rocking Bonedale!

And last, but of course not least, to each of you who will read this book, thank you for joining me. May the process plant a seed in your heart and soul. As I tell my clients and students, "Never give up your dreams. Dance your fear and imagine the possibilities!"

Contents

MILE MARKER 1
MILE MARKER 2
MILE MARKER 3
MILE MARKER 4
MILE MARKER 5
MILE MARKER 6
MILE MARKER 7
MILE MARKER 8
MILE MARKER 9

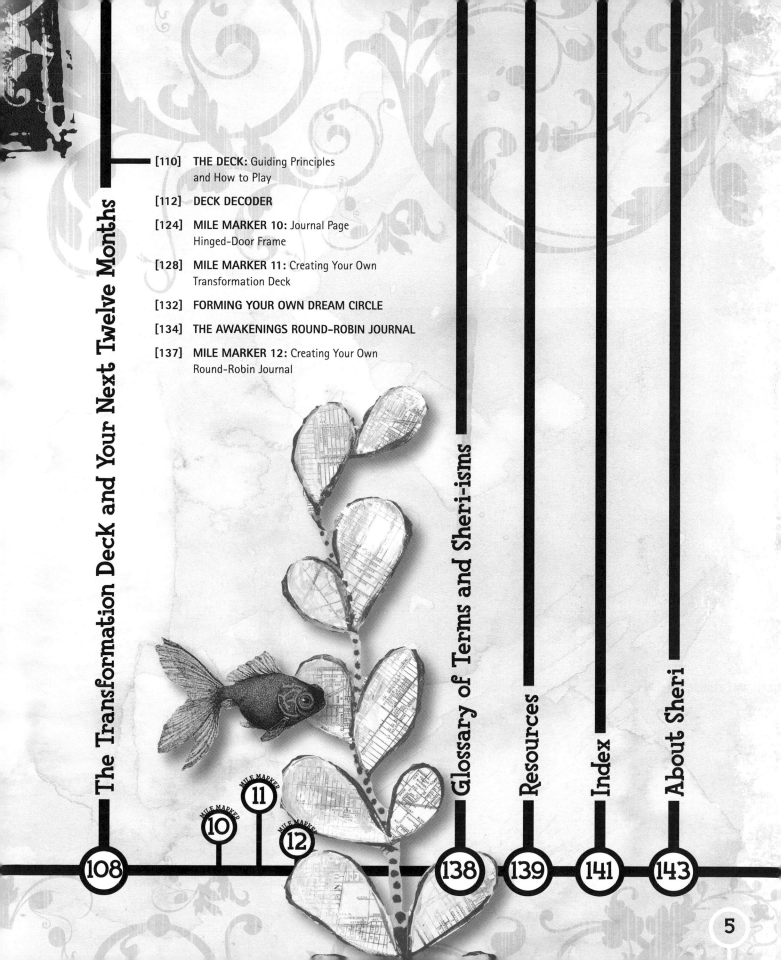

The Adventure Begins
Fate Might Lend a Hand

Awakening: 1. a moment in which clarity or insight is gained.

I offer you this story, the origins of finding my authentic self and of knowing I could no longer play it safe. I share with you the seeds of this book and the adventure of my life. It was 2001, and I was adrift; my inner compass was broken. I was going through an early midlife crisis of sorts. My career path had not been a linear one. There was not going to be a thirty-years-of-service gold watch for this woman. In the realm of life callings, it always seemed like there was one more magnificent opportunity just over the horizon. I had no regrets about any of the choices I had made in my life, as out of each of them, a challenge or opportunity grew. But I was the most disillusioned I had been in a long time.

I had already experienced several career incarnations: photojournalist, rubber-stamp mail-order artist and T-shirt designer. Alongside each of these was an ever-steady paycheck received from work as a psychotherapist. It was the psychotherapy career that was weighing on me at the time, and although I had tried to bring the arts, as a healing element, into my work with clients in mental health settings, I was yearning to create the practice I had always imagined. I was out of alignment with my values and true beliefs about how to help people. My work was beginning to feel like an old itchy skin that no longer fit.

The problem was that every time I attempted to shed that old skin or think about what might be next, what I refer to as the Venomous Toad Committee would croak up its fears and what-ifs. To keep me towing the line, the committee would round me up and lead me to the edge of the cliff for a view of the BIG BLACK BOTTOMLESS VOID—land of the unknown. Inevitably, I would run screaming from the edge, back to the safe career with benefits.

As a life and creativity coach, I believe there comes a moment in our lives when we have to ask the age-old, yet important question, "Am I truly living the life I have always imagined?" Or to paraphrase the poet Mary Oliver, "If I could put fear and doubt aside, what would I really want to do with this one precious life?" What if I followed my heart, not my head? One day—without really knowing it was on the way—that moment came for me.

In September, the Twin Towers crumbled, my family lost an old friend in the tragedy and, as a native New Yorker, the event hit my psyche in a way I did not expect. We were living to work, our priorities felt skewed, and there was little time to support the people we loved. I had submitted a proposal to open a wellness and healing arts center in an old home my husband and I were going to purchase. The house had it all—three-car garage out back for studio space, several rooms for practitioners and even room for a healing garden out front. In the end, the city planners denied our proposal, citing, "not enough parking." I was absolutely crushed; it was, for me, the final blow—compass glass cracked, dials pointing nowhere. I came home in tears and said to my husband, "What now?" He answered, as he often does, with something that immediately elevates my heart rate. "Why don't we just get out of here for a while—hit the road for a year?" "*What?*" I stammered. "That isn't what I meant at all!" And that, my friends, is the moment the course of my life was altered forever.

Over the next few months, we bought a twenty-four-foot travel trailer, learned the language and skills of RV life, discarded most of our possessions, packed up what was left, and rented out our home. It was a whirlwind and I have to say, I was still not convinced; I was *terrified*. Let's remember the timing: Our country was living in fear. Each day we were being told to trust no one, to look at our neighbors as potential criminals and enemies and to be alert at all times for new dangers. Was it a yellow, orange or purple day? How could life change so drastically in an instant? The bombardment of messages wore on my soul like sandpaper.

When we broke the news to friends and family, the reaction of each person we told was like a Rorschach test of my risk-taking stamina. Parents: *You're going to do what?* Grandma Elsie: *You always were a free spirit. Go follow your heart!* Friends: *How can you quit your jobs?* The Toad Committee: *What are you thinking? Your private practice was just starting to be on an even keel.*

What did I do? I drew from my inner resources. I knew that I had faced the unknown before and THRIVED! At different times over the course of my life I had faced addiction, a divorce and moving away from everything and everyone I had ever known. Now, here I was again, facing the unknown, but somewhere deep inside there was a very tiny voice saying, "This one small step has the ability to change everything. Just believe and keep walking forward."

So we did. In September 2002, we pulled out of our driveway with our beloved fourteen-year-old lab and hit the road for a year of adventure and personal transformation. It's a great story, but that's for another book. What I will tell you is this: During that year, I was stripped down to the core and my authentic self was revealed. By the end of that year, I knew exactly what I wanted to do with the rest of my life and I was no longer willing to deny it. By diving head first into the unknown, I was able to step fully into the life I lead today.

Before we left on our trip, I facilitated two workshops in our area, using (with her blessing) Carol Lloyd's book, *Creating a Life Worth Living.* With Carol's permission I designed and added expressive arts and journaling exercises to her process. The teaching bug took hold. When we arrived home, I knew I could no longer live inside the traditional box. I created an intention to become a live-your-dreams coach and workshop leader. I would design my own curriculum, but I had almost no idea where to start. I began with a single question, "What do I believe about teaching women to realize their dreams?"

Asking myself that one question opened the door to imagining new possibilities for my life.

Creative Awakenings is my answer to that one very powerful question. Within these pages, I hope you will begin to ask some questions of your own and glean some answers in response.

As with most dreams, this book began without my knowing it, as a tiny seed in my heart. *Creative Awakenings* is a workshop in a book, based on a class and retreat I have been teaching for almost ten years called "EnVision the Life of Your Dreams!" The class supports clients and students in uncovering, discovering and creating a vision for their lives and businesses. For many participants it's the first time they can share a dream aloud without someone telling them it's impossible. As a result, our groups become safe havens, a cheering squad if you will, filled with DREAM SPIRIT! I will be your dream ally, workshop facilitator, outfitter and cheerleader, from afar.

Creative Awakenings will invite you to honestly ask and answer your deepest questions. It will give you a safe place to begin to imagine the life you truly want to create, a way to look beyond what you can see now with creative exercises, tools and techniques to use along the way. Your journey begins here in this moment. I invite you to let the chatter and negative voices fade away, and allow your heart to open to the possibilities this experience will offer.

Like you, I have walked many miles along life's highways, through some treacherous territory, along slippery slopes. It is my deepest hope that this book will make your journey a little smoother. There is a story inside you, waiting to unfold. The seeds of your dreams lie dormant, awaiting water, sunlight and nourishment.

Blessings for the journey.

– Sheri

The Calling

What in your life is calling you?
When all the noise is silenced,
the meetings adjourned,
the lists laid aside,
and the wild iris blooms by itself
in the dark forest,
what still pulls on your soul?

In the silence between your heartbeats
hides a summons.
Do you hear it?
Name it, if you must,
or leave it forever nameless,
but why pretend it is not there?

— The Terma Collective,
"The Box: Remembering the Gift"

Don't you just love that poem? The spoken expression of the words feels like a psalm. It is a powerful statement and one most of us can relate to. The first time I read this poem, it took my breath away. I had been hearing the calling for some time yet turned a deaf ear, out of fear and insecurity. The first stanza of this poem offered me an opportunity to know I was not alone in my desire for something different, something that would nourish my soul. *What is calling you?* allowed me to hear the question inside me, "If I could I would. . .". And that question reverberated with my heartbeat for weeks. It was, in fact, the beginning of knowing I could no longer play it safe for fear of "What if?" The poem was the key to unlocking the doors of my heart. I hope *Creative Awakenings* will offer you just that, a key to unlatch the doors to the deepest places in your heart. Places you may not have allowed yourself to visit for a long, long time for fear of the consequences.

I come from a long line of dreamers, so perhaps it was inevitable that I would eventually find myself here. It began with my great-grandparents, immigrants who left Russia to come to America in search of a better life. As I look back through the generations, I see how each person planted their dream seeds, gave them water and a whole lot of sweat equity, and brought their dreams to fruition. I spent many hours and days in the fields of my

family's dreams. My grandparents on both sides were entrepreneurs, and my mother and father each created their own businesses. My younger brother named his dream at age sixteen and I lived to see it manifest in the most extraordinary way.

I honor those who have walked before me; I have witnessed their determination and their resulting passion and joy. So, it seemed natural that I would grow up to reach for my own. From this vantage point, I see clearly how the roots of my family tree gave nourishment to my life's dreams. For most of my life I have used art and visual journaling to tell the stories of my soul, and to sow the seeds of my own dreams.

Your journey begins here in this moment. I invite you to let the chatter and negative voices fade away, and allow your heart to open to the possibilities this experience will offer. Unless we take risks to grow, we can never reach our full potential.

It is my deepest hope that this book will make your journey a little smoother. There is a story inside you—the seeds of your dreams, dormant—waiting to unfold.

And when the calling begins, as a whisper or howl, THIS IS THE PLACE TO START.

Resist the temptation to breeze through the writing to get to the pretty pictures and the step-outs. Take your time . . . read—simmer—play—create.

Gearing Up (Supplies for the Journey)

It's time to get packed for the adventure! As with most trips, it's important to have good, sturdy materials to take with you on the journey. Remember, we don't have to have the most expensive gear to have a great adventure. Very often, practical, affordable and sturdy gear is already available in your closet, garage or kitchen!

Substrates

A primary substrate you will use for this journey is a 9″ × 12″ (23cm × 30cm) spiral-bound, hard-cover, sketchbook journal to create your Book of Dreams Journal (see page 12). Other substrates and surfaces you will see in *Creative Awakenings* include: Clayboard, cardstock and papers of all kinds, particularly those in a travel theme.

Adhesives and Mediums

For my Book of Dreams Journal, I use a glue stick. It's not archival, but it's great for quick collage and stream-of-consciousness journaling. Découpage medium or acrylic gel medium can be used for both gluing and sealing. Soft matte gel medium is great for photo transfers of all kinds, and liquid matte medium works well to extend or thin your paint—more bang for your buck!

Field Note

Placing wax paper between your journal pages that contain glue, paint or gel medium will keep them from sticking together.

Color

Craft-grade paints are inexpensive and offer a great way to get your feet wet, eliminating the "it-has-to-be-perfect" mentality. They come in small bottles and a great selection of colors. Save the artist-grade paints for your archival canvas pieces.

Golden Acrylic Glaze Colors are fabulous. They add a hint of color yet remain transparent, allowing what is below the color to show through.

Gesso is a primer and can be used on almost any-thing—paper, canvas, hardbound book covers. It will give interesting effects both as a first coat and over the top of an altered surface.

As for brushes, I get mine at the hardware store—all shapes and sizes.

Cutting Implements

As an adventurer, I always carry a pocket knife. In ad-dition, I recommend scissors of all kinds, a craft knife (change your blades often for nice, easy cutting) and a cutting mat.

Mark Making

Mark making is an ancient form of communication. On many of my river and hiking trips, I have been privileged to see petroglyphs (drawings and symbols carved into rock and cliff dwellings), left by travelers before me. These images have had a big impact on my art, so I use all sorts of things to create lines and marks on my pages. A few of the items in my collection include pencils (graphite sticks, charcoal sticks and traditional sketching pencils—often sold in a kit), gel pens, water-soluble crayons, oil pastels, waterproof pens all kinds, waterproof India ink, as well as objects and implements for scratching into the surface.

Camera

The Photojournalist Creed: Keep a camera with you at all times; you just never know when that perfect moment will appear! I have 35-mm film cameras from my photojournalism life that I will never part with. I have also been known to use my grandfather's twin-lens Roliflex, which created many of the vintage images you will see in this book. But, for the most part, I shoot digitally now.

For important, high-resolution shots, I use a Canon Digital EOS-D60. A digital pocket camera is always in my bag for daily excursions. A Holga camera is another fun way to play with alternative photos (see Resources, page 139) but it can be a little pricey to develop the film if you don't have a darkroom.

Found Objects and Ephemera

I love alternative magazines from big magazine stands. I adore the wild, colorful and random images. I use these magazines in my Book of Dreams Journal and not in pieces for sale. As an adventurist, I am an avid collector. Memorabilia of all kinds finds its way into my studio: leaves, rocks, sticks, labels, menus, flyers, shells, beads, glass, metal and other found detritus.

Hitting the Road: Adventure Packs Prepare for a Gypsy Spirit Day

I love Gypsy Spirit Days (see page 117)! When I travel, I always bring a journal and some art supplies, so when the muse tickles my heart, I am ready to meet her. Over time I have acquired duplicates of my favorite items for my adventure packs, so I don't have to spend excess time finding things. Looking for stuff—as you know—is often a major deterrent to the creative process. Therefore, my adventure packs are always ready to go out the door at a moment's notice. I have two packs to choose from.

Day Pack

For me, this is small; it is my grandmother's funky old makeup bag. I take this with me when I travel to distant lands, usually when a plane is involved. Inside is a small gouache or watercolor kit, pencils, pens, glue stick and a collection envelope to store found ephemera. (I store my tiny scissors in my checked bag.)

Weekender

This pack is one I throw in my car for weekend excursions. It is an old 1950s-style hard shell makeup case I found in a secondhand shop. What's inside? More of the same except with these additions: inks, calligraphy pens, random rubber stamps, ink pads and a small bottle of white gesso. There are a few different-sized inexpensive brushes as well.

Think about what supplies you'd never want to be without, but try to keep it simple, and then put together your own adventure packs.

Field Note

Art supplies can be hazardous to your health. All items included in this supply list and in the artist's demonstrations are suggestions only. Be mindful of your health and read all labels carefully before deciding to purchase or use any supplies in your studio. Always work in a well-ventilated area or outside when possible. Personal Note: I use either latex or nitrile gloves when I work. (Years of work in the darkroom with bare hands have made my skin and lungs pretty sensitive.)

① The Book of Dreams Journal

What You Need

Having rounded up your gear and started preparations for your journey, your first task is to create your Book of Dreams Journal. You will use this journal with "The EnVision Process" (see page 18).

Your journal will hold all your intentions, dreams and field notes to help you create a vision for your life. You will also use your Book of Dreams when using the Deck of Transformation enclosed in this book (see page 112). It will become a visual and written guidebook, a place you can visit over time and return to, especially if you feel you have lost your way.

A few words about my own journals. My Book of Dreams Journals are rough-and-tumble—kind of like me—all muss and no fuss. I want them to be a place where I can work intuitively. I spill my intentions and dreams to the page without worrying about perfection or the end result. I don't always *want* to *know* where I am going. I want to see what unfolds, what is beneath the layers—basking in pleasant surprise. On my pages, you'll see bubbles, blobs, tears and spills—the rough edges that make up my dreams.

Using our intuition is a big piece of reaching for our dreams. Dreams are not tidy; they can be random, and sometimes wild, so I invite you to let go and trust. Take risks, make a mess. In the end it really doesn't matter. What we want is to unlock the door, to have the Universe dance and play with us. If we get caught up in the details, the outcome or how it looks, we might miss out on a truly extraordinary discovery.

- scrap paper
- 5″ × 5″ (13cm × 13cm) sheet of aluminum (TENseconds Studio)
- foam mat or a piece of suede or leather
- stylus
- assorted embossing templates
- paper stumps
- quilter's wheel
- wire brush
- alcohol inks
- palette
- foam applicator
- paper towels
- gel medium
- glitter
- spiral-bound journal (Canson)
- white pencil
- craft knife
- wax paper
- gesso
- acrylic glazing liquid, satin (Golden)
- Patina Green glaze (Golden)
- Phthalo Green, Blue Shade acrylic paint (Golden)
- tape
- paste paper or decorative paper

On a scrap of paper, create some sort of symbolic drawing of your own (it can be very simple) and center it over the back of the aluminum sheet. Working on the foam mat (or a piece of suede) and using a pointed stylus, trace the image. (Remember, what you are tracing on the back will be reversed on the front side.) Set the aluminum on the first embossing template you wish to use and burnish it with a paper stump tool, as if you were doing a charcoal rubbing.

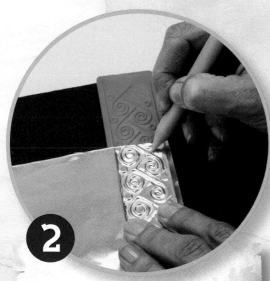

After you can see the general pattern, emboss the detail a bit further with a smaller stump.

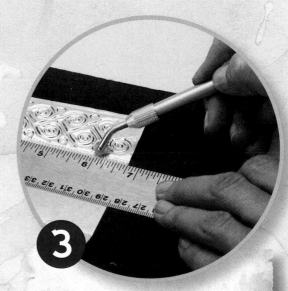

Repeat the pattern on the other side of the sheet. Use a quilter's wheel to create a dashed line inside both halves of the patterned area.

4

Use a small wire brush to give some texture to the center portion. Continue embossing from both sides, as you see fit, using a stylus to sharpen details when necessary.

5

You are now ready to add color to the metal. Squirt some of the alcohol ink onto a palette and then pick it up with a felt applicator and rub the color on. Start with one color and rub it on. (Use a paper towel to blot excess ink and smooth out uneven areas.)

6

Continue building up layers of color until you have the look you like. Apply gel medium to an area of the metal where you would like to have some glitter, and sprinkle some over the wet medium.

7

Tap off the excess glitter and apply a second color of glitter if you like. When the gel medium is dry, scrape away any glitter that may be on areas where you don't want it. Apply additional medium over the glitter to seal it.

8

When the piece is dry, position it on the front of your journal where you would like it to be visible through a window (which you'll create in the next step). Trace around it using a white pencil.

9

With the cover open and placed on a cutting mat, use a craft knife and a metal ruler to cut along the lines. Be mindful to not overcut the corners. Open the journal to expose both the front and back covers and put wax paper under each. Cover the boards with gesso. Crumple up a paper towel and create texture over the gesso to disguise the brushstrokes.

10

To get between the spaces of the coil, lift the board up to the coil as much as possible and brush right over the wire and onto the board. Don't worry if you get gesso on the coil; you can wipe it off when it's wet, or scrape it off when it's dry.

11

Let the gesso dry. Make up a mixture of equal parts glazing liquid and Patina Green glaze. Brush it randomly over the entire cover, blotting off some of it with a paper towel. I like the color to be a bit more concentrated in the corners. Brush on a mixture of Phthalo Green, Blue Shade and liquid glazing medium to intensify the color a bit.

12

Let the journal dry thoroughly. Apply tape to the back of all four sides of the metal piece so the sticky side is facing up.

13

Position the metal under the cutout window of the journal and press the cover to the tape to attach it.

14

Turn the cover over and burnish the tape well to the cover. Cut a piece of paste paper or decorative paper to a size just slightly smaller than the dimension of the front cover. Adhere the paper to the inside of the cover using gel medium. Adhere a second piece of paper to the inside of the back cover to complete.

Charting the Course
Looking Back So We Can Go Forward

What's the first thing you can do with your Book of Dreams? Begin by answering these questions.

1 When you look back, how do you honestly feel about the last year of your life? Where were you successful? What were your life or business challenges? (Personal, financial, etc.)

2 What are your creative and personal strengths?

3 When have you been honored and valued for doing what you truly love?

4 Name three specific areas of your life or business you would like to impact by using this book.

5 If you were completely honest with yourself, what limiting or false belief might be holding you back from stepping into your dreams?

6 Imagine I have given you a magic wand; it has the capacity to remove all your fear and doubt. Close your eyes, wave the wand and *presto:* You are free! Now that you truly believe your dreams are obtainable, what will you reach for this year?

7 Are you ready for the creative adventure of a lifetime?

"In the silence between your heartbeats hides a summons. . . DO YOU HEAR IT?"

The EnVision Process
Creating a Vision of Possibility

In recent years, popular culture has embraced the idea of the Law of Attraction (see Glossary, page 138). This philosophy generally states that thoughts become things (so choose them wisely). This idea is not really a new one; it has actually been discussed for a long time. I think what has changed is that people are now ready to hear it and *embrace* it.

One of the first books written about this concept was *As a Man Thinketh*, written in 1902, by James Allen. Spiritual teachers like Dr. Wayne Dyer, Shakti Gawain and Christian Northrup have been talking about this concept for years. If you are familiar with the Law of Attraction and are using that in your life already, you may enjoy bringing the EnVision Art of Intention Process into your practice as well!

Why Intention and Not a Goal?

Goals have a definitive place in our lives and businesses. I use them all the time. They can be very beneficial for things like writing a business plan, applying for a loan, reaching a deadline, etc. However, the main objective of a goal is the *end achievement* or *aim*, as the dictionary tells us. When discussing this concept with students and clients, I have found that very often this linear and masculine *aim* is what keeps us from giving ourselves permission to dream or see new possibilities for our lives. If we see the *goal* and can't see anything between it and the here-and-now, we might have trouble envisioning how we will get to the end result. It makes sense to me, as I have been in exactly this spot myself.

Here's what I mean: Imagine you have a bow and arrow in your hands and you are aiming at your target. Can you see the bull's-eye? What else do you see in your view? Probably nothing, as you are completely focused on the center circle, thus limiting your view of anything else in your sight. You may also notice you have stopped breathing and the muscles in your body are tight and rigid, because you are so focused on hitting the center of the circle. Would you know if someone was coming up behind you right now? Inherent in a goal is a succeed/fail message, and if we don't hit the bull's-eye, we can feel like we completely missed the mark.

Creating an Intention

To create *intention* is to *create a vision of possibility*. Intention is the union of aspiration, intuition, vision, personal action, synchronicity and sprinkling of alchemy. Intention invites you to take in the expansive view—broad, receptive and wide sweeping.

I believe the key to separating an intention from a goal is the word *intuition*. In modern culture we are increasingly disconnected from our innate inner wisdom and intuition. We are so plugged in that we have tuned out what is inside. When completing a goal, we generally have a defined series of steps that will help us get to the end result. By remaining focused on those steps, we may cut ourselves off from our own intuitive knowing.

With intention, we have the desired result in mind. Instead of relying on a specific list of steps to get us there, we are tapping into our intuition—our inner wisdom—to help us find our way. In doing this, not only do we see the target and the bull's-eye, we are able to take in the full panorama! When we take in this larger view, it allows us to be open to change, new possibilities and synchronicity that may not have been a part of the original vision.

The beauty of intention is this: In the end, you might discover where you thought you were going isn't exactly where you ended up. Yet when you look at the new view, you notice some of the original pieces are very much in place and some very unexpected pieces are there as well, because you allowed yourself to take in the full vista of possibilities. Let's take this one step further. I think this idea will be one we can all relate to.

The Blank Canvas

"Dreams are like the paints of a great artist. Your dreams are your paints, the world is your canvas. Believing is the brush that converts your dreams into a masterpiece of reality."

— Unknown

As an artist, I fell in love with this quote—a perfect metaphor for creating intention in our daily lives. Creating an intention is like starting with a blank canvas. When we begin, there is nothing we can see. We go inward, tapping into our intuition, knowing that with small, determined strokes, we will begin to see what is possible. At first it might not be perfectly clear—it might be a rough sketch.

It is at this exact moment—when the lines are unclear—that self-doubt can enter the picture. Because we can't see the end result clearly, disbelief and judgment will often move in (without paying rent), leaving us wondering if there is anything inside worth painting at all.

If we have no tools to work with this particular challenge, this one moment of doubt is just what the Toads (negative voices in your head), gremlins and naysayers have been waiting for. They raise their voices shouting, "Who are you kidding? This is impossible!" And for many of us, this is the point of surrender.

As your workshop facilitator, I say, "This is no time to stop—KEEP GOING!" Grab your brushes and favorite paints! It is time to use bigger and broader brush strokes, bolder colors. I beg of you, give the dream breath and light. Please don't shove it back in the box! You might not be sure how you will get to the final masterpiece, but with each stroke of the brush or pen, the picture *will* become clearer.

The Masterpiece

Think of your life as a beautiful blank canvas, awaiting your attention, color and brushstrokes. As you dance with your canvas, you will observe the beautiful panorama, noticing surprising elements and the smallest details. As you add these new pieces to your canvas, your masterpiece will be revealed.

If you are still uncertain, come dance with us as we delve deeper and explore new paths on the remaining pages

"Name it if you must, or leave it forever nameless. . . but why pretend it's not there?"

of this book. Keep reading and you will discover the EnVision Art of Intention Process can help you create a beautiful vision of your life to come.

Travel Tips
Helpful Hints for the Journey

There are many different ways to use this book. The beauty of *Creative Awakenings* is that you will benefit from some or all of it. You can travel page-by-page or take the full cover-to-cover, twelve-month voyage. How you choose to get to the destination is, as always, completely up to you. I have written a few travel tips as a guide to help you get started.

Travel Tip 1: A simple and restorative place to start is by reading about Everyday Bliss on page 118 and incorporating this daily ritual into your life. The benefits of this one activity will offer you the ability to uncover the seeds of dreams and ideas, help them take root right now, and give you an opportunity to add creative play into your daily life.

Travel Tip 2: You can take a solo flight or invite one of your friends to be your Dream Ally (see Glossary, page 138). You can also connect to others using the book and activities at the *Creative Awakenings Discussion Salon* at www.creativeawakeningscommunity.com

Travel Tip 3: One of my favorite aspects of travel is the magic of not having a completely outlined plan. It allows room for spontaneity and magic! You can incorporate this into your *Creative Awakenings* adventure by closing your eyes and opening the pages to "see" where you find yourself on that particular day.

Travel Tip 4: Group creative play! This book can be used as a guidebook for your *Creative Awakenings Dream Circle*, to enhance a book club, for girl's night out or to inspire creative thinking in your office or organization.

You are about to embark on a very personal and exciting journey. This creative exploration and adventure will take you to lands once traveled yet perhaps forgotten, and roads walked but not fully explored. Are you ready? Grab your hiking boots (or step into your favorite pair of cowgirl boots) and pick up your journal, pencils and pens. There is no more time to waste. Join us—it's time!

The Process, Step-by-Step
Practice Living Your Dream

The explanation of the EnVision Art of Intention Process holds many answers to your questions. This process was the foundation of the twelve-month collaboration you'll read about in the following section. All of the contributing artists began with this simple and powerful practice.

There are three steps to The Process: EnVision DreamTime (a relaxing experience to help you identify your intention), The Art of Intention (an intuitive process to help you create a vision in your Book of Dreams for the intention you uncovered in your DreamTime) and Reflections (taking time once or twice a week to interact with your art-of-intention piece, using writing and additional collage).

Step One: EnVision DreamTime

It's time to envision your dream! EnVision DreamTime is like any new skill or practice, it will take a little time and patience to allow your body, mind and spirit to learn this new rhythm, dance to the new beat and allow your heart to sing. Remember, practice—not perfection. Just dream.

Like guided imagery, DreamTime is a deeply relaxed yet interactive state of consciousness. During your DreamTime you will ask yourself a series of questions. Any question that steps away from fear or self-judgment is appropriate. Your questions can be specific to your dream, project or concept, or they can be general in nature. Here are some examples of questions you might explore.

General Questions

Where does my heart truly want to go this month?
What would I do if I knew I could not fail?
What would I do if money were no object?

Specific Questions

What needs to happen this month in order for my business to grow?
How can I allow more creativity into my daily life?
How can I better understand the challenges that are holding me back?

You Will Need

your Book of Dreams Journal (see page 12)

candle

soft music—almost inaudible

magazines

personal photographs

glue stick

your favorite paints, pens and collage supplies

Field Note

Make the first Monday of each month your EnVision Dream-Time Day. Place this date on your calendar with a DreamTime sticker to indicate nothing will come between you and your dreams!

Create a sacred space by lighting a candle and playing soft, calming music. This will signal your mind that you are moving out of your everyday routine and set the mood for inner exploration.

Close your eyes and begin taking some quiet deep breaths in through your nose and exhaling noticeably through your mouth.

Allow any thoughts or pressures from the day to float away. This is your time, a time for going within, listening to your intuition and creating space for your life dreams. Hint: If you are struggling with letting go of the day, imagine a beautiful container with a lid labeled *For Tomorrow*. Place your concerns inside and close the lid. This will give your mind permission to relax, as you are letting it know you will come back to the container when it is time.

Take another deep breath and ask your question. Remain relaxed and aware. Don't worry too much if you don't get an immediate response the first or second time you try this. I promise something is happening, even if you don't get complete clarity or a definitive answer; ideas are bubbling and percolating. Some of us will come out of our DreamTime with a clear answer, others will find it in the art-of-intention journaling process.

When you feel ready, open your eyes and pick up your Book of Dreams Journal. It's time to create your art of intention. Hint: You will be tempted to write, but don't go there yet. Writing now will move you over to your linear mind and I want you to stay in your receptive, creative mind.

Field Note

If you would like support to relax during your DreamTime, I have created a DreamTime Guided Meditation CD-ROM especially for this book. It is available on my Web site at www.sherigaynor.com

Step Two: Creating the Art of Intention

Creating the art of intention will serve two purposes: It will allow you to create an intuitive, spontaneous, visual image that reflects your intention, and it will help you intuitively uncover and discover intentions that are still hazy and not quite clear.

Now that you have taken some time to go inside and uncover your intentions and dreams, it is time to work in your Book of Dreams to *set your intention*. What do I mean by that? As I said earlier there are times when we can't clearly imagine the picture or the intention. I believe that in order to know where we are going, we need a definitive visual aid, something that we can see in our mind's eye, guiding each step we take along the path.

Images are there to empower us. They arrive to share stories in a way words cannot. Images speak to our right brain, the receptive half, that holds the key to our creative essence. Our receptive and imaginative brain is where the art of intention lives. Creating visual imagery will help you cross over the boundary of your left-brain, intellectual knowing (also known as our Ego), allowing access to unconscious archetypal material. It will also let you "set" the intention by revealing the intention or dream to your subconscious mind and announcing it to the world!

At this point, you might think you're ready to put this book down, and you may be saying to yourself, "This won't work for me. I am not an *artist*."

WAIT! Hold that thought and please read on before you make that decision.

The only rule in this book is, there are no rules.

When I found out the word "art" was going to be in my title, I balked and felt a bit panicked. I know many of you aren't afraid of this word at all and art is a big part of your life, but I was really concerned about alienating the art-a-phobes—those who still believe they don't possess an ounce of creativity.

Many potential students call me to inquire about a workshop and, in a whisper that is barely audible, lament, "I want to try your class, but I am terrified. I don't have a creative bone in my body." I quickly slip on my creativity-cheerleading cape and lovingly coach them past this common, limiting belief. Generally, these exact students are the students who creatively explode, as if giving them permission to step through the door of the studio allows them to uncork the creative fire quietly smoldering at the core of a smoking volcano!

So I would like to take a moment to talk to those who might be willing to use the exercises, but not delve into the "art" (i.e., creative) activities.

"Take part in a journey of the imagination in a nurturing and supportive environment where there are no rules and anything goes. Don't let the word art *scare you. . . . Absolutely no creative experience is required!"*

This proclamation is the theme of my coaching and creative workshops. It was borne out of my own personal experience, when I, too, believed I was not an artist, because I could not draw.

If you have ever used your imagination to raise a child or develop something new—this can be as simple as rearranging your home or altering an old family recipe—you are using your creative marrow. Have you ever lost track of time while gardening in the yard? Time has no meaning when we are connected to our innate creative essence. It has to do with connecting with spirit and source, the one inside us and the one that guides us. In many cultures there is no word for art. This tells us everything we need to know about creativity and how it lives inside *each and every one* of us, not just a creative elite. We are all creative beings. It is only in recent history that we have chosen to take the word "creativity" and make it something that is beyond ordinary men and women. In doing so, we have shut down the gift we have inside each of us to reach into our core and tap into something that is not tangible—creative alchemy. In creating art of intention, you are going to take an intuitive trip into the mystery.

Creativity is your birthright!

Back to the art-of-intention process! I will often use a timer when creating my intention. I give my students about fifteen to twenty minutes for this part, so they know to work fast and stay receptive.

Gather your Book of Dreams, the magazines, personal photographs and collage ephemera. I often work over the space of a two-page spread. Even if you use only one side of the spread, your writing (see *Step Three: Reflections,* page 24) will be on the opposite page. Close your eyes again and take a deep breath. You will notice how easy it is to slip back into the relaxed state.

In your mind's eye, imagine the intention or dream you discovered during your DreamTime. Begin sifting through the magazines, personal photos and ephemera, allowing the images to speak to you. Don't question or judge the images; they all have something to tell you. They are not "good or bad, dark or light." Simply rip them out as they speak to you, even if they are repulsive or you don't understand them. A great trick to keep you from reading the articles is to hold the magazine upside down. Focus on color, movement, texture and figures.

Place the images in a pile as you work until the timer rings. Spread the images out in front of you and set the timer again for fifteen minutes. Working fast, and without over-thinking things, reach for the first image that speaks to you and begin your collage. *No scissors!* Why? Because scissors will get you caught up in the details. It will keep you from entering "the zone," the deep meditative state that occurs when you are ripping the paper. I know this sounds funny, but I promise you, it changes everything!

A glue stick works great for this process, allowing you to work fast and without much left-brain activity. Add in elements of your own, such as drawings or personal photographs. This is pure catch-and-release for your soul.

Embellish! Once you have completed your collage, feel free to embellish with paints, stamps or pens. Make it your own. You can put a wash of gesso over the image and doodle and paint your heart out. If you did not find a clear answer during your DreamTime, the art-of-intention can be used to help you find clarity. *Something will be revealed* to you, even if there was not perfect clarity! Go to the next step; your answers may be there.

Step Three: Reflections

When you are finished with the collage, date the piece so you have a reference. Use the next page or the adjoining page in your journal and, as you reflect on your piece, *spill your thoughts* onto the page.

Over the course of the month, take time at least once or twice a week to interact (sit with, look at and pay attention to the thoughts and feelings that emerge) with your art-of-intention. As you do this, transformations will occur and new questions or answers will arise. As the changes occur, feel free to add new imagery to the piece you created in the beginning of the month. You can also create a larger piece from the original idea, or create a new art of intention piece using this process again as things shift. As with any guidebook, continue to make notes and references about what you have discovered.

Congratulations on taking your first steps toward claiming a life filled with passion and purpose! Having now experienced The EnVsion Process, you have laid the groundwork for the rest of our time together.

Any good outfitter will chart the course, provide provisions and offer instruction to support you in carrying out a successful journey. I can help you find direction, but it is up to you to commit to the journey.

Committing to the Adventure

Here is your next challenge. In the beginning of any adventure, there comes a time when you have to commit to the journey by applying for a visa to visit the new territory. I have incorporated your visa application right in the book (see page 27). A visa affirms your intent to travel. The Creative Awakenings Visa is a contractual affirmation, offering you the opportunity to give yourself the time to truly commit to this personal expedition.

Do you ever hear yourself saying to friends, "I just can't seem to find the time to be creative. Between my job and my family, it just keeps getting put on the back burner"? Oh my goddess, did you just feel a little pinch in your solar plexus? That probably means you can identify with this statement as being true for you.

Committing to the process and staying the course may be difficult for you, so I am going to offer you a challenge: Let *Creative Awakenings* became your CREATIVE MANDATE.

I know we are all frantically busy, and the idea of a twelve-month creative practice might feel like another weighty to-do, so I have created a couple of different visas to choose from: The twelve-month or the thirty-day. As with most visas, the dates of the journey are your choice. You can apply for the specific period of time suggested, or create your own time frame. Remember, you can always apply for re-entry!

When heading out on a journey, none of us will start on the same road or ocean. In a similar way, each of us will come to this journey with different life stories and experiences, as well as readiness and risk tolerance. Some will be completely ready to leap and others will need to take baby steps. Some will experience a series of small *aha* moments, others will have the light bulb go off. There is no *correct way*. The point is we all learn from one another and experience growth. It's all part of the fun! What I will say is this: Never fear. Transformation can occur without completely unraveling your life as you currently know it!

Travel Tip
A Little Note About Leaping into Voids

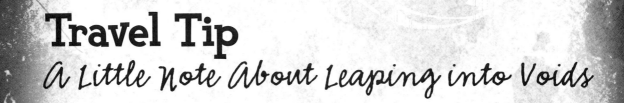

> We shall not cease from exploration;
> And the end of all our exploring
> Will be to arrive where we started
> And know the place for the first time.
>
> "Four Quartets"
> — T.S. Eliot

A client shared this quote with me and I absolutely love it. The metaphor of the journey in the T.S. Eliot piece reminds me of the transformation that occurs as we take the risks to explore and, as we do so, shed the old skin that will reveal the new moist shimmering one.

Although I am now more comfortable leaping without a parachute, I was not always this way. It has taken me almost twenty years of small, calculated leaps to be able to quickly assess the level of risk, and very often my Venomous toads still share their feelings. The difference now is we have a much different relationship.

My suggestion for exploration: KNOW THYSELF. If you were born with wings, by all means leap and soar. But if you are more like I was when I first started leaping, find a good support system to help you evaluate the leap so when you land, you are on solid terra firma.

② The Visa and the Milestones Passport

The Visa

The Voyager: The 12-Month Visa

Before embarking on our twelve-month voyage, I strongly recommend applying for the visa. If you were planning a trip around the world, you wouldn't want to rush the process would you? You would want time to fully experience and savor the places you will visit and the people you will meet.

I know what you're thinking, "*Twelve months*? Is she crazy? I can't even find time to do my laundry. How am I supposed to dedicate twelve months of my life to envisioning and creating my dreams? Clearly she doesn't know what *my life* looks like!"

I completely empathize! To be quite honest, I was actually right there with you the day I received the contract for this book! I had no idea how I was going to juggle this project with the rest of my life commitments. And that, my friends, is exactly how the visa was born! So, I am walking my talk when I ask you to consider this idea.

If it's any consolation, in hindsight, the year I spent writing this book was the most empowering year of my life! I am not going to tell you it will be effortless, but when has anything worth having ever come without some perseverance, a slight change of attitude and some major sweat equity? What if the *Creative Awakenings* practice isn't another to-do? What if this is just the opportunity you need to slow down and *be present*? What if you give yourself a gift this year—twelve months to imagine the possibilities of your life?

The Expedition: The 30-Day Mini Visa

If you are still feeling timid about applying for a twelve-month visa, I suggest applying for the mini-visa, with a minimum stay of at least thirty days. When exploring a region, it's suggested that you take at least thirty days to capture the true feeling and sense of place. If you can manage the time, six to twelve weeks will give you an opportunity to soak it all in, learn the language and embrace the customs.

To change any habit we must fully embody the new lifestyle, so we feel the changes on a cellular level. Most behavioral specialists will tell you it takes at least thirty days to break or embrace a new habit.

Like any solid guidebook, suggestions are made for places to visit, but inevitably the road is yours to travel in any way that suits your style. Is there a way to navigate the challenges and find safe waters? Don't take the signing of this visa lightly; let's go on an inner exploration.

Once you have signed the visa, you will have all the tools you need to join us in the adventure of a lifetime. This was your last preflight mile marker!

Field Note

When choosing the specific amount of time you would like to commit to this adventure, what objections show up? What challenges or obstacles might come up to delay your flight? Before you choose your dates, write the positive affirmations and solutions for each objection and each challenge.

The Creative Awakenings
Visa Application

Purpose: To visit uncharted territories of creative adventure

Dates of your journey:

The Voyager: 12-month visa: Check here: _____

The Expedition: 30-day mini-visa: How many days will you be committing to your adventure? (Minimum suggested stay is 30 days–12 weeks)
Insert your dates here: _____

Re-entry dates: _____

I _____, of sound mind and heart, am ready to begin a new adventure. In doing so, I commit to giving myself the full benefit of the *Creative Awakenings* process. I will start by putting myself at the front of the line of my creative life. I will make time to do my assignments and engage in my daily rituals. I will commit to the mystery of this process and, though I might be somewhat apprehensive, I will learn to work with my resistance. I understand that change means taking risks. I commit to understanding that even the simplest change leads to experiencing something different. I know that by signing this visa, I may introduce new challenges into my life, regarding prioritizing and old ways of being in the world.

I sign this contract, doing so with a full heart, ready to take even the first step to uncovering my deepest desire. I commit to taking small steps toward my dreams, knowing that living my most authentic life can take a little time. I understand that nothing worth having comes immediately. I understand that in simply allowing for the room to believe, I can create something different in my life. I will train my mind to see the possibilities and not the challenges and obstacles. I commit to working a daily practice, even if I feel like I don't want to or have not completed an assignment, as I understand that this is fertile ground for me to gather more information. Most of all, I commit to allowing myself to believe that the possibilities in my life are endless and that creative solutions exist for me.

_____
Signature

_____
Date of Entry

The Milestones Passport

Woo hoo! Let's celebrate! You have filled out your visa and committed to the journey, and by now you've been working in your Book of Dreams. Now it's time to make your Milestones Passport and begin your adventure!

This passport is your tangible representation of the adventures you have lived and the roads you have traveled. It is a discernible validation of your willingness to be bold and adventurous. Using your Milestones Passport will allow you to create a visual stamp of celebration for each step of your journey. Bring it in your purse or day pack (see page 11) to catalog your experiences. Collect items and ephemera from the trip and add them to your passport when you return home. If you have applied for the mini-visa, use the passport to document and celebrate your success during your chosen dates for adventure.

Maybe you will want to use your passport with the Deck of Transformation activities (pages 108–133). Pull a card each day and use the exercises to lead you where you need to go. When you have completed the exercises, create a Milestone-of-Celebration page in your passport. You can use the passport any way you like, celebrating each and every step of your *Creative Awakenings* adventure in any way that suits your personal style.

What You Need

- 8½" × 11" (22cm × 28cm) white cover-weight paper, about 8 sheets
- 9" × 12" (23cm × 30cm) colored cover paper
- ruler
- awl
- pencil
- binder clips, 2
- bookbinding needle
- bookbinding thread (waxed linen)
- wax paper
- brush
- gel medium
- travel maps or other decorative paper of your choice
- barren (optional)
- small photo of yourself
- self-adhesive photo corners
- assorted gel pens, markers, paints or any other art-making materials of your choice

1

Fold each of the white sheets of paper in half. Use a ruler to find the center of the fold on the cover piece, and make a hole with an awl. Make two marks on both sides of the center hole, about 1½" (4cm) apart, for a total of five holes along the fold.

2

Stack the folded white pages together and center them with the colored cover. Secure the pages and cover together with two binder clips.

3

Turn the stack over and use the awl to make holes through the white pages, using the holes already punched in the cover as a guide.

4

Thread the needle with about 18″ (46cm) of thread. Keeping the booklet clipped together, number the holes with pencil and the left and right corners, as shown here: Upper left, lower right, hole one in the center, two and three going left to right, four to the left of center and five as the first hole. Starting in the center hole, thread the needle from the outside of the booklet to the inside.

5

Leave about 6″ (15cm) of thread on the outside and thread the needle through hole number two and back up through hole number three.

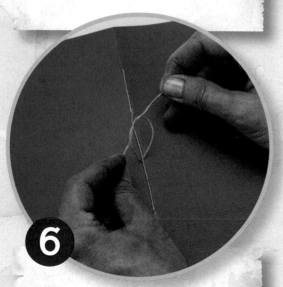

6

Thread the needle back through number two, and come up through number four. Then go through hole five to the outside, back up through hole four and back through number one. Turn the book over and make sure all of your stitches are taut. Tie a knot.

7

To begin altering the inside of your passport, open it to a spread and put pieces of wax paper behind the pages you'll be working on. Using a brush, apply gel medium over both pages.

8

Adhere map images (I scanned and printed these out) to the wet medium. I like to use a barren to smooth the paper down, but you can just use your fingers if you prefer.

9

Add a photo of yourself to the page. (To create your own "Rockstar" portrait, go to the Discussion Salon at www.creativeawakeningscommunity.com for directions.)

10

Add some color around the perimeter if you like, either with acrylic paint or glazing medium.

Field Note

I like putting the fortunes from my fortune cookies into my journal sometimes, but I often doodle on them first.

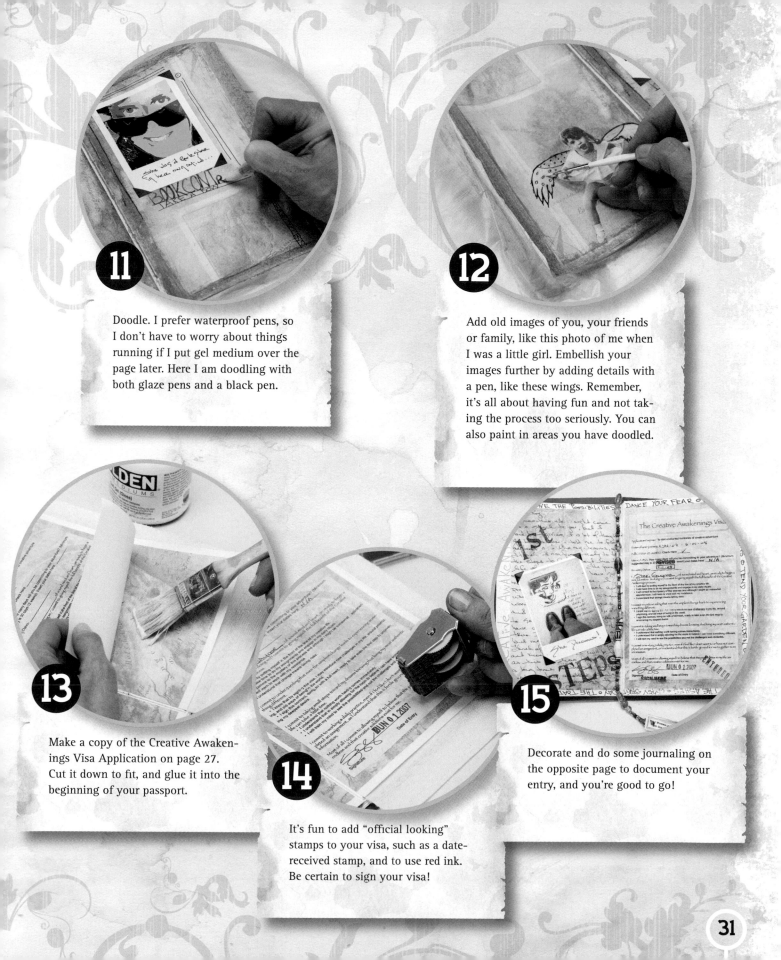

11 Doodle. I prefer waterproof pens, so I don't have to worry about things running if I put gel medium over the page later. Here I am doodling with both glaze pens and a black pen.

12 Add old images of you, your friends or family, like this photo of me when I was a little girl. Embellish your images further by adding details with a pen, like these wings. Remember, it's all about having fun and not taking the process too seriously. You can also paint in areas you have doodled.

13 Make a copy of the Creative Awakenings Visa Application on page 27. Cut it down to fit, and glue it into the beginning of your passport.

14 It's fun to add "official looking" stamps to your visa, such as a date-received stamp, and to use red ink. Be certain to sign your visa!

15 Decorate and do some journaling on the opposite page to document your entry, and you're good to go!

Twelve Months of Dreams
The Art of Intention

In June 2007, I invited eleven artists to join me on a yearlong journey centered around the art of intention. Each artist picked a month to engage him- or herself with the EnVision Art of Intention Process. They were given an artist's packet describing the process (see page 18) and asked to create a mixed-media art piece based on the intention revealed to them during their DreamTime Session. (See Step One: EnVision DreamTime, page 21.) The artists were not assigned intentions or topics; they created their intentions from their own experiences, desires or needs.

During their chosen month, each artist was to interact as often as possible with her art of intention piece (see Step Three: Reflections, page 24) and keep a journal of her experiences. Finally, each artist wrote a personal essay, sharing her experiences using the EnVision process. A collaborative project called the Awakenings Round-Robin Journal, (see page 134) traveled from artist to artist as well over the yearlong period. The Awakenings round robin involved pulling a card from the Transformation Deck and creating a small collage and an exquisite corpse (see Glossary, page 138), then writing in the round-robin journal based on the card they received.

As you will see when you read the artists' personal stories, *Creative Awakenings* is less about technique and more about creative process and personal transformation. You will see the artists did not follow a rigid, cookie-cutter set of steps when setting their intentions and working through the process—each did what felt natural to her.

We were aware that the roads could get muddy, mile markers lost, and inevitably, there was a chance we might lose our way. We committed to the mystery and a personal exploration, knowing any adventure worth having always involves challenge and a healthy hint of danger.

Our mantra was and remains: *It's the adventure, not the destination; process, not perfection!*

As you follow along with us through our twelve-month journey, you will see journal entries from my personal Book of Dreams, depicting my transformation over the year's time. You will also see entries and letters, written on the once-private blog, to the artist contributors who were invited to form the *Creative Awakenings Dream Circle*. The full twelve-month story can be found on the now-public blog at the *Creative Awakenings Discussion Salon* (see Resources, page 140).

In this section, we have also provided several art-making techniques for you to use during your adventure. Some may be familiar to you and others may not. If you find a technique familiar, we invite you to break out of the box and find a new use for it. How could you apply it to your creative process in a totally new way?

It is my hope that as you see the wide range of approaches to The EnVision process, you'll see there is more than enough room for your own style. I hope you'll be encouraged to share your own experiences with others, just as these generous artists have agreed to share with you.

Sheri's blog entry

It has been a busy few months of traveling and teaching in new and familiar venues. I have flourished in the gathering of like-minded creative souls. The experiences have allowed me to feel I am on the right path and my heart is filled.

It is my day to dream—to EnVision and create my intention for the month. As the designer and outfitter of this project and process, it seems only right that I lead the way. In wilderness language we call this breaking trail. The pieces of my long-term dream are in place, and yet a huge part of me is completely terrified. Not surprisingly, I find myself in the same place I see many of my clients and students—facing the Abyss, the Mystery, the Void. Call it what you like, it's that BIG, DARK, SCARY place where there is no concrete or visible answer. The place we all wish we had a reliable gypsy, with a trustworthy crystal ball. My work is a co-creative process and as such, it is my true belief that the teacher always has more to learn, so I will find a way to start and embrace the concept known as beginner's mind.

So many questions are running through my mind, the internal chatter is deafening. The Venomous Toad Committee is shouting its fears. "Who do you think you are? What if you can't pull this off? You are a coach; you are supposed to have it together. Now you're going to share your vulnerability? What are you thinking?" And they continued. . . "A year is a really long time. What if the artists decide they don't want to do the project when it is their month to dream?

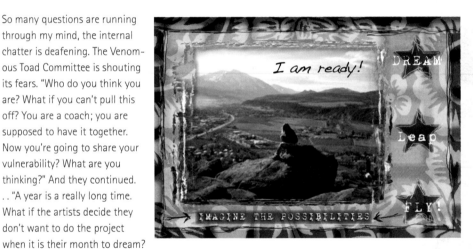

Is your art even good enough?" The pressure is enormous and I must find a place of serenity, or I will call my editor and tell her I can't go through with it.

I take a hike up Red Hill to clear my head. I feel a bit of vertigo and discomfort as I climb out on the edge and sit on an outcropping overlooking my beloved town. The metaphor is not lost on me. The view before my eyes is majestic Mount Sopris. At almost 13,000 feet, she is my sacred touchstone. As I gaze at her two peaks of ancient rock rising solidly from the earth's core, I feel a sense of inner peace. Symbolically this mountain is my grounding, my True North. In the next moment I shout at the top of my lungs to the valley floor below, "I AM READY!" And in that moment I realize I must start at the beginning and tell the story of how this all began, the journey where my own personal transformation took seed. I set up my camera and hit the self-timer; it feels important to document this moment.

I return home and sit at my desk. From deep inside I hear a voice that says, "Walk your talk, use the process, live what you teach." With a racing heart and trembling hands, the writing begins. I gather my courage and lean hard into my fear, trusting that just beyond what I can see at this moment, a colorful rainbow is waiting to greet me—a place of synchronicity and possibility, a place of dreams and trusting the process.

June Dreamer
Sheri Gaynor
Beginnings

When your compass is broken, you might have to set out without one and use the stars as your guide.

Setting the Intention

I will embrace the mystery! I will be *fearless* and LEAP into the void!

Today I will take the first steps to living my ten-year dream by celebrating the successes of the last few months. I will commit to writing and creating art from my soul. Here is my twelve-month intention. I will give this project my personal best, knowing that in the end, that is all I can do. The rest is unknown to me at this present moment. I will attempt to deal with what shows up over the next twelve months with love, intention and grace, knowing in my heart that I don't always know what is best for me. I understand there will be joyous moments as well as tough times, and that this is the rich fertile soil we call life. I will. . . TRUST THE PROCESS! This month's intention: Be Fearless, Leap into the Void!

Journal Entry:
June 10, 2007

(See *Tend Your Garden*, page 119.)
Yesterday I went to my favorite nursery. The employees there are so helpful and kind, even during spring frenzy. I feel a sense of hope after winter's long, dark nights as I see the first crocuses bravely poke their heads out of the barren earth, the first gifts of spring.

All week I have been using seeds, plants and weeds as metaphors with clients. It seems so cliché and overused, but I know why—it's completely appropriate. Our creative souls are truly such fragile entities. Trusting our gifts and talents can be difficult in the face of criticism and potential rejection. Our dreams are the same way. They are not to be taken lightly but nurtured until they are ready to stand tall on their own. It is important to protect our dream seedlings, so they are not inadvertently mowed over by a careless Dream Bandit. (See Glossary, page 138.)

This book is a seed, a long-held dream, awaiting sunlight and water, yet I find myself almost paralyzed now that it has manifested. Signing the contract was an experience in itself! I even had to assign the task of completing the book to someone in the event of my untimely death. That experience was like the exercise where you write your own epitaph—humbling and profound.

Journal Entry:
June 12, 2007

(See *Shadow/Light*, page 113.)
I was reading M.C. Richard's *Centering: In Pottery, Poetry and the Person*, yesterday. This is an out-of-print favorite that I re-

turn to when I need to remember to return to my own center. I take a breath, ask a question and open the book to wherever the spirit guides me; it's fun, somewhat like a daily meditation book.

Yesterday I opened and read this: "Human beings are an odd breed. We find it so difficult to give in to possibility—to envision what is not visible." It is so interesting that the word EnVision was right there. Out of 160 pages, I was led to the class I have been teaching for eight years that supports women in uncovering and stepping into possibilities for their lives.

I believe M.C. is talking about the polarities that we create within our lives and ourselves. These polarities set up limiting beliefs and also untruths about who we are in the world and what we truly might be able to accomplish for ourselves.

I know in my own life that my polarities tend to have their roots in fear, competition and judgment. This has become an old way of being in the world and over the years I have chosen to move to a new model, one of cooperation and collaboration. In doing so, I have met some of the most amazing women. Women who are generous, loving and caring. Women who will stand by your side and cheer you on when life gets hard. They provided me with a beautiful model of love, communication and above all, integrity.

Blog Entry to Artist Contributors: June 23, 2007

I may have stumbled unexpectedly onto our twelveth participant. It is a magical story and I will let you all know tomorrow if she says "Yes." I know we were calling in a male, but no one has shown up at this time. I think I understand why. Thomas,

you are going to be carrying the torch for the masculine. It is all just perfect. Keep your fingers crossed for me.

Blog Entry to Artist Contributors: June 30, 2007

What surprises me is that in setting my intention this month to birth and grow our book to the best of my ability, new paths have been shown to me that were completely unexpected. Some have been exciting, others painful yet transforming, forcing me to wake from a deep slumber. I am not ready to reveal these potential changes, as I want to sit with them and tune into the voice that appears to be calling. It is still small enough that I am not sure what it is saying, but my intention for July is to slow down enough to listen and see what it might be asking of me.

Blog Entry to Artist Contributors

Dear Fellow Dreamers,

When I reflect on the month of June, I understand that symbolically it was about New Beginnings. I am not surprised. In many ways writing a book would have to be about beginnings reaching toward an end. On June 1, 2007, I set my intention for the month: Be FEARLESS. . . LEAP! Lean into the fear and just begin, take one step to manifesting your long-held dream." To be honest, at that moment I felt completely overwhelmed and somewhat paralyzed, knowing I was starting on the project much sooner than I anticipated, due to our approval and manuscript deadline. In my mind, I saw the project beginning on September 1, which would have given me time to sort out some of the details in a less harried manner. The best laid plans are often upended and quite unexpected!

As artists we often face deadlines and each of us have ways in which we engage with the pressure of this task. My process around deadlines—and it took me awhile to understand it—seems to be to wait until almost the last minute, the ideas simmering until the pressure builds and the pot is boiling over and the work comes pouring out of me. So the pressure I felt to start was not an unfamiliar feeling, it was just that the stakes felt much bigger and I was well aware I was going 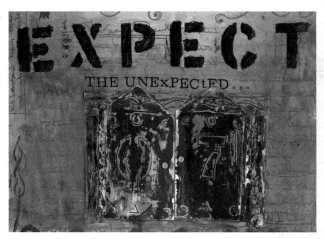 to have to do it a new way. I was launching my dream, a seed that has been awaiting water for a long time.

Setting my June intention to be fearless, breathe and lean into the fear also became my mantra for the next year. I also recognized that I would need to find a way to balance the writing process with my already-filled plate, so this was a truly holistic and transformational experience and not another weighty to-do. When I realized I would be leading the way for our Dream Circle, I also realized that many of you would be feeling a similar pressure with your active and busy lives, so I would like to share the intention I have created for myself around this book with all of you. When your packet arrives. . . take a breath. Open your artist's packet with the intention of slowing down. Come to the process with a clear mind, and not as another "to-do." Engage in the month you have chosen with an open heart, and not in stress and overwhelm. I invite you to give yourself one day, one hour, one moment to breathe and ask what it is you truly want to bring forth in your life. What is the small voice that whispers to you in the middle of the day, that wakes you in the dead of night, that tickles your soul and has the potential to rock your world? What would it be like to take a moment to hear it, to acknowledge it, to engage with it? This month's intention: Expect the unexpected!

July Dreamer

Susan Tuttle

To Dance Requires Balance; To Balance Requires Dance

Calendar numbers (partial, shown vertically): 13 20 27 · 12 19 26 · 11 18 25 · 10 17 24 31

Seeking balance in life involves finding and embracing the delicate balance between destiny and free will; knowing when to act, and knowing when to let go. . . and that is the ultimate dance.

— Susan Tuttle

My plate was full. I was attempting to juggle more than your average jester when Sheri invited me to participate in her book. My reactions: honored and excited, then a bit panicky, as I had no idea how I was going to deliver. As a stay-at-home parent of two young children, and as an author working on her own first book, I had a lot of responsibilities. Yet, I knew I could not pass up her offer. I trusted my gut feeling, and am so glad that I did, as this experience has changed my life forever.

Setting the Intention

Lighting a scented candle, my mind raced with thoughts that went in many different directions. The flame of the candle was centered and still. I imagined myself becoming that flame. My mind and breathing began to slow and I became more observant of my thoughts. I asked myself, "What is it that I need?" I began to think of all of the roles that I play in my life with all of the projects, jobs and responsibilities. Being a perfectionist, I want to do everything well and I can also be my harshest critic. Often biting off

more than I can chew, I think a part of me really enjoys the challenge. As I continued to write in my journal, following my first EnVision session, I realized how I bring things that I love into my life, and I can honestly say that there is nothing in it that is unwanted. The only problem is that I want to do it all at once! On the flip side, when I look back at the extremely busy times in my life, they have often been the most productive.

Here's the stream of all of my roles and responsibilities in no particular order: mom to two little kiddos, wife, artist, author, friend, businesswoman, play dates and outings, cleaning, social commitments, errands, e-mails, blogging, art shows, art submissions and teaching. After making this list, a word presented itself very clearly in my mind: *priority*. As I began to think about my priorities, it became clear that they fell into two tiers: The Big Picture, where my family is my first priority and writing my book is second, and a second tier, Moment-to-Moment. Priorities in this second tier are in constant flux— especially with having kids. This is where I need to decide what is most important in any given moment.

Incorporating the Creative Process

Creating an art piece symbolizing my intention to bring balance into my life had

bal'ance, *n.*, *v.*, -anced,
-ancing. —*n.* 1. instrument
for weighing, usually con-
sisting of two scales. 2. equilibrium. 3. harmonious ar-
rangement. 4. act of bal-
ancing. 5. remainder, as of
money due. —*v.* 6. weigh.
7. set or hold in equilibrium.
8. be equal to. 9. reckon or
adjust accounts. —bal'anc-
er. ...

its moments of ease and moments of uncertainty. Immediately I knew that I wanted to incorporate my favorite apple tree—the one at the end of my dirt road that I see almost daily. I've seen it with the most resplendent, full harvest moon behind it, watched lightning streak across the skies above it, observed it with full lush leaves and sweet-smelling apple blossoms, and witnessed its limbs heavy with ripe, red fruit. I've seen my tree barren and exposed as the temperatures turned chilly, then blanketed in crisp, white snow, asleep for the long winter. To me this tree represents perfect balance—stoic and accommodating to its environment. It bends in the wind, can survive a broken limb is deeply rooted, while at the same time flexible. In a vision for my art piece, I wanted to somehow incorporate the image of my face with the trunk of the tree—to symbolize an aim for creating perfect balance in my life.

The digital portion of my piece (the melding of my face into an image of the tree, using photo-editing software) developed very smoothly. However, when I adhered the digital photo to my canvas and began applying color, I ran into trouble. I attempted to use bright, vivid colors and combined them in several ways, none of which worked. I was about to walk away from the canvas for a while when my three-year-old son came over to my paint bin, filled with at least fifty bottles of paint, and handed me a bottle of pink, saying, "Mommy, use this." I obliged, and started to get excited, as the colors seemed to finally be clicking. He proceeded to give me two more bottles, one light yellow and the other blue. I worked those colors into the substrate and added a hint of mint green. His artistic decisions were so right-on and pointed the piece in a completely new direction—exactly the direction it was meant to go. What an amazing synchronistic experience! My son beamed that day in the studio when I praised him for all of his artistic help. Since that moment, he spends most afternoons with me in my studio, the two of us painting away as his sister takes a nap.

By setting my intention to bring balance into my life, and creating an art piece to set that intention in motion, I have done something very powerful. In the past I would set intentions on a more subconscious level. I knew what I wanted to bring into my life and I would go for it. Until now, I have never clearly declared intentions in a conscious way. By performing conscious intention setting, I believe I am bringing more awareness, clarity and understanding of what I intend to manifest.

Meditations on Balance

Balance—to me, it's about being centered and rooted, so that choices can be clearly seen and understood, and decisions can be made with awareness, understanding and compassion.

Internalizing

Something that is becoming clear to me on this journey is that I internalize so much of what goes on in my environment—whether it is good or bad for me. I think a certain amount of internalizing is a good thing; it means I am a thinking and feeling human being. I do not wish to be desensitized to my environment. I cannot watch much news for the same reason. I tend to internalize the tragedies I witness, often becoming depressed over them. I realize it is good to be an informed citizen and care about the state of the greater world, but I must learn when to turn the television off, as well, so that I do not allow myself to become overly engrossed in tragedies.

The Transformation Deck

It was time to work with the transformation deck and create my piece in the Awakenings Round-Robin Journal (see page 134). I drew the *Tend Your Garden* card. I was happy to get this card, as it was in synch with my state of mind at the time. I had been thinking about the lessons in life that I was meant to learn; how I was meant to grow in this life that I have as Susan Tuttle. As I go through this process, I realize that learning "balance" is definitely one of the lessons. It is all about choosing my path (what I want to learn and how I will do it, with help from the universe of course). Each time I get closer to learning the lessons—to evolving—I feel a sense of coming home. My piece in the Awakenings Round-Robin Journal is representative of this sentiment.

On Resting and Running

In order to lead a balanced life and to have enough energy to move toward my intentions, it is so important that I take the time to rest. I often push myself too hard, using up every last ounce of energy, and then sometimes even trying to push past that threshold. I may feel like I am making more progress, but in actuality, I am making less, and even setting myself back. I am trying something new these days—changing my ways since embarking on this quest for balance. I am resting when I feel tired and taking the time to play and do things for me when I can. In terms of working on my book and pursuing other artistic endeavors, "even keel" is a much better route for me. If I imagine myself as a runner, I would be a long-distance one. Sprinting is just not for me; that would zap my energy and require recovery time. "Long-distance running" involves pacing myself: doing a little bit of work on my book and art endeavors each and every day. That work happens mostly in the evening hours, after the kids and hubbie are all asleep. If I feel on top of things with my work, I feel content and stress-free, and thus I am able to be a much better mother to my kids during the day.

Sitting on Things

One morning, during the EnVision process, I received a whole batch of important e-mails that required me to make some difficult decisions and then respond to the senders. My immediate reaction (which tends to be a pattern for me) was to come up with responses quickly, to get the issues out of my hair, so that I could have a clean slate, empty of responsibilities for the day. Balance? I think not. I am learning that when I make quick, split-second decisions in this manner (don't get me wrong, split-second decisions have their place and can be useful) it does not serve me well. It is better just to sit on these things for a half-day, a day or even overnight. When the dust settles, I mull over the e-mails for a bit (or whatever happens to be the matter that needs attention), the decision I need to make comes into focus and there is clarity in what I need to do. If I react too quickly, I often have regrets and wish I would have responded differently. I also find that e-mails often read very differently the next day.

When it comes to decision-making, I am working on following my intuition, trying to cultivate the wisdom of knowing when to respond quickly or when to sit on it for a while.

Who's at the wheel anyway? Well, I am, technically, as I truly believe in free will. But I also believe the universe has a big part in it all. Let's tap into my belief system for a moment. I believe our lives are a balance between free will and destiny. You ask, how do I know this? Well, it is a feeling—actually, more of an instinctual knowing—that I have. I surely cannot tell you exactly how it may work, nor is it my job to try and prove my beliefs, or even impose them on you. I am just sharing what I know to be true.

Here is an analogy: Birds will migrate south for the winter (for me, this is symbolic of destiny), and how they choose to get there, what their stops will be along the way, what they will choose to eat, and so on, represent free will. So, what does this dance between destiny and free will mean for me in my life and how does it relate to this "balance" I am intending to bring into my life? It means: 1. I need to have an awareness of myself, others and my place in the world. I must be open to and aware of what I am meant to learn and do in this life. 2. In using my free will, I need to consciously work toward manifesting my intentions—my spiritual work to evolve my soul, so to speak. (Translation: no sitting on my butt waiting for things to happen.) 3. I need to realize what is out of my control. What can I let go of? Part of that involves listening—listening to my heart and listening to my inner voice, even listening to the universe when it may want to take me in another direction than what I originally thought. 4. I must have complete and utter trust in a loving universe that has my best interest at heart.

So, in a nutshell, seeking balance in life involves finding and embracing the delicate balance between destiny and free will, knowing when to act, and knowing when to let go—that is the ultimate dance.

③ Merging Digital with Mixed Media

For her intention piece, Susan first created a piece of digital art and then manipulated the finished image further with color applied by hand.

What You Need

digitally enhanced photo of yourself

water-soluble pastels

damp cloth

gesso

glue stick

decorative or found paper

acrylic paints

paintbrush

pencil (optional)

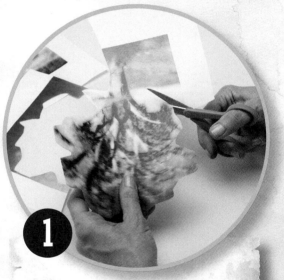

1 Print your photo out and cut out the portion you wish to use.

2 Alter the photo with water-soluble pastels.

3 Lightly blend the pastels with a damp cloth.

4

Cover the background around the cutout portion with gesso, blending the outline of the cutout into the paper background at the edges.

5

Add pieces of decorative or found paper to the background to create a landscape. Fill in more of the space with acrylic paints.

6

Add some background paint around the outside of the cutout to begin blending it with the background. Also bring some of the colors of the background into the photo.

7

Add back some detail lines with pencil or pastel.

8

Spatter watered-down paint onto the piece by knocking the paint-filled brush against the wrist of your other hand.

Sheri's blog entry

As we move into the dog days of August, I am in awe as I look back over July: Expect the Unexpected. No matter how many years I have been doing this work, I still wonder at times how our days can be so filled with such extremes of shadow and light occurring at the same time. In her book *The Places That Scare You*, Pema Chödrön would say, these are "two sides of one coin. . . an interesting, smelly, rich, fertile mess of stuff. . . when it is all mixed up together, it's us, humanness."

Last night Susan Tuttle and I had our interview. Susan was the first of the invited artists in our Dream Circle to work the EnVision process. Listening to her journey during the month of July had the startling effect of bringing the book to life for me—interesting as my intention this month is about initiation.

I was transfixed as Susan read me the journal entries she had written over the month. She could have never known that many of the experiences she had were experiences my students have had over the years. In many ways, Susan walked the steps of the class, without having a manual! How is that for synchronicity and magic?

Susan immersed herself in the EnVision process. I feel so much gratitude for her grace and enthusiasm. Because I am not sure who has this address at this time, I am not going to share deeply about our personal experiences. I am going to just post tidbits and teasers. When I asked Susan if she would use the process again, she said, "Oh my gosh! Every day for the rest of my life!" And with that statement, I tell her I feel my heart expanding and she has helped me to believe that I am creating something meaningful to give to the world. My August intention: Believe!

August Dreamer
Katie Kendrick

Creativity as a Vehicle to Self-Discovery in the Present Moment

My intention was, and continues to be, to become more mindful in the living of my life, and to discover how holding that intention, to become more aware and present to the moment-to-moment details and various aspects of my life, impacts and informs my creativity and art making.

When I received the invitation from Sheri to join the group, I was immediately curious about the project. Because I admire and respect the work Sheri does—as a creativity coach, a group leader, a teacher and an artist—I felt this opportunity may be something I didn't want to miss out on. At the same time, I was already feeling stretched to the limit with a number of other upcoming projects and deadlines. I needed to be careful not to take on more than I could handle. Protecting the quality and pace of life keeps me healthy and sane, as well as allowing me the time to put in my best effort and follow through with the commitments I make in a timely manner. Keeping all these things in mind, I thought it still couldn't hurt to just hear more about the project. I believe the universe is continuously presenting us with opportunities to learn, stretch and grow in the exact ways we need. The more Sheri told me about the EnVision process and the accompanying project, I could feel the excitement building in me and the more certain I became that this wonderful opportunity was meant for me.

I had a sense about what my intention would be before I got off the phone with Sheri, even before I did the DreamTime exercise, although I followed her directions anyway, being open to any new intention that might sweep ahead of the one I already carried with me. But even after lighting the candles, sitting quietly for several minutes, then throwing my questions out to the universe, the same answer came back to me: Focus on mindfulness. My intention was, and continues to be, to become more mindful in the living of my life, and to discover how holding that intention, to become more aware and present to the moment-to-moment details and various aspects of my life, impacts and informs my creativity and art making.

It seemed like such a huge and extremely broad intention, one that I knew at the time I could attain only imperfectly at best. But it was also one that was the hinge upon which all my other goals and art-related aspirations rested. I wondered how my motives and ambitions might change and evolve when examined with the clarity of non-judgment. I wondered which of the notions I carry might fall away, and which ones would rise and shine brightly as being true to my authentic nature. This was going to be an interesting adventure.

My intention for the month is to be in the present moment

MOON

YELLOW

sunflower and seeds

When I see the yellow sunflower and the yellow moon, immediately my spirit feels lighter. The moon reminds me to look up, into the vastness beyond me, a beacon it reflects light, just like the sunflower just makes me happy those big bobbin head birds

I do and can now the me happy those big the birds at the small area

Once I had clarified my intention in my mind, I journaled about it using words and paint on a large gessoed atlas page, which is where I do most of my visual journaling. I found myself emphasizing key words and phrases and creating them in bigger, broader script—concepts like *being awake, non-judgment, compassion for myself, curiosity.* These were touchstones of how I wanted to approach creating my mixed-media intention project. They were also reminders of how I could maintain enthusiasm for my intention after multiple times of lapsing back into forgetfulness.

This is a project that would inform me about myself, and remind me to keep my heart soft and compassionate when the rise and fall of thoughts and emotions would come bursting to the surface. This was especially helpful with troublesome areas like feeling blocked, insecure or inadequate. My fluctuating mood swings have been extremely challenging at times, but because of them, I have also experienced grace beyond my comprehension and the capacity to feel gratitude for all my experiences—because I wouldn't be the human being I am without them.

I am a self-taught artist in that I have no formal art education, but I continue to enjoy taking classes from artists I admire and feel drawn to whenever I can. The reason I create art is because it is one of the most potent ways I have discovered to connect to the infinite and dynamic flow of the universe inside myself. Period. I have a deep longing for that spiritual connection, and working from my heart is what fuels the creative process of my art making. I practice listening and playing intuitively, trusting the creative process in my heart, even when—especially when—my mind doesn't see the logic, doesn't understand where the whole thing is going and feels like a lost traveler in a strange land. In the process, in the very personal adventure of repeatedly "letting go," I have an opportunity to meet myself anew, to get to know the real me, the one that too often remains hidden behind thoughts and thinking, memories of the past and worries of the future.

I wanted my art of intention piece to remind me to stop, breathe and take in the reality of the present moment. I felt this piece needed to be a combination of painting and collage work united to a collection of objects of personal significance—objects I could physically touch. This created a reminder of concrete, physical reality when I was feeling airy and ungrounded by racing thoughts and whirling feelings.

I decided to house the project in a treasured gold gilded box that was made in Italy, one I was fortunate to find on one of my hunting forays at a local thrift store. I took the cover off its hinges and used the open box as the stage for my piece. From the beginning, I never had a plan or "big picture." It's just not the way I work. Instead, I trust each step will lead me to the next, and it never fails to do so.

The collage elements I chose to use for the background were a combination of three personal photographs I had taken, and I used them in the form of glued paper, transfer and transparency. Each of the photos I used contained personal symbols I often use in my artwork: a moon, tree and door. I combined the moon at night with the daylight scene below it to remind myself that there will be times when my world feels dark and un-navigable and I can't seem to find my way; other days I will feel clarity and a sense of direction. The full moon in the night sky brings several things to mind: a light in the darkness, the mystery and vastness of space surrounding all the objects in the universe, including that that is within me, and the changing "seasons" of each month that reflect my often-changing moods.

And doors, while representing an entrance to the comfort, safety and security of home, also represent new adventures, passages to personal or universal truths, and gateways to mystery and unknown dimensions of consciousness. A door symbol reminds me to remain curious and awake to the now, the only place where aliveness exists.

When I think of trees, I think of solid creatures, rooted to the earth, their branches either bare or covered by leaf "skins." They are creatures that can bend and ride on the invisible wind—a safe harbor to birds, providing a place for them to grow, live and sing their joyous songs. Whenever I walk in the woods, it's easy to leave my thinking, projecting and worrying behind and simply enter the present moment. To experience nature's beauty in all its stages of birth and decay and align myself with those rhythms, that beauty, is a way to come back to myself.

After creating my mixed-media background, I typed out personally meaningful thoughts and phrases of well-known Buddhist monk Thich Nhat Hanh, a humble yet powerful man I consider to be one of my beloved teachers. The phrases I glued around the perimeter of my collage include: *don't be attached to the future, live the actual moment, be aware of your breathing, recognition without judgment—see reality as it is, all is a miracle* and *only this actual moment is life.*

Next, I gathered a collection of found objects—my representatives of concrete physical reality. These would help ground me in the intention to be present. I gath-

ered them without thinking, I chose them instead by their feeling of familiarity and how I experienced the world and myself when I looked at or touched a particular object. At the end of the process I had selected a stone and a sprig of alder cones (both items I had picked up on the ground in our woods by the river), a small cascade of translucent beach glass collected and given to me by a dear friend, and a tiny glass vessel that holds a small and fragile bright yellow blown glass flower, also a gift from a friend.

I spent time arranging and rearranging my collection at the base of the box, feeling content with my choices, yet enjoying the process of picking each item up, holding it in my hands and moving it around to find its resting place. As I moved pieces, thoughts wafted through my mind of dear ones, peaceful times spent in the forest and along the banks of "our" beloved river, the calming sound of the water, the songs of the birds, the glint of sunshine reflected on the water, the rustle of the leaves in the wind. . . memories enjoyed in the present moment that my touchstones bring to the now.

As Sheri suggested, I placed the finished artwork in a prominent place—my kitchen—where I was guaranteed to see it several times a day. As the days passed, I noticed that each time I walked into the room and saw it, I remembered to take a deep breath in mindfulness, and often even two or three. In the breath, I could feel the stillness I experience when I walk in the woods or along the river, the peacefulness in my being. I feel a strong sense of gratitude for the opportunity to be a part of this very "enlivening" project, and for the grace that supports our intentions.

Artist Katie Kendrick's work embodies art as a vehicle for self-discovery. Here Katie shows you how to create rich, luscious and personal layers to take your art of intention to a new level.

What You Need

- assortment of papers
- journal page or other paper
- acrylic paint
- gesso
- brush
- pointed object like the end of a brush
- watercolor crayons
- damp paper towel
- charcoal pencil

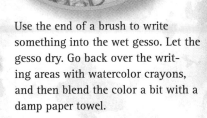

Glue torn scraps of several types of paper down to your journal page or other paper. It's more interesting if some of the papers have text on them, and others have different prints and patterns. Mix a small amount of the acrylic paint of your choice with some gesso. It's OK to not mix it together completely—leave a few streaks. Use a brush to apply the mixture around your collage elements.

Use the end of a brush to write something into the wet gesso. Let the gesso dry. Go back over the writing areas with watercolor crayons, and then blend the color a bit with a damp paper towel.

Outline some of the textured areas with a black charcoal pencil.

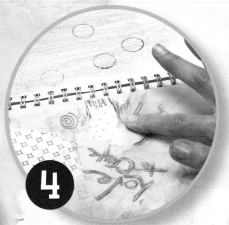

Blend the charcoal in a bit, using your finger.

Sheri's blog entry

What an amazing month August was. I honestly don't know where the summer has gone. I am not quite ready for fall and the layers of clothing it will bring. I love feeling warm sun on my skin and the earth under my bare feet.

August was a time for retreat and belief. Suffice it to say, it was a much-needed break to ground myself and move into a completely new rhythm of life. The yurt experience was HUGE—I mean ENORMOUS—and I have been soaking in every moment of these two weeks I took off from my practice. Do you know what? I have not taken a full-on, two-week vacation in years! This summer I set an intention to do what I teach, slow down, write and enjoy the season! I am walking my talk and I honestly think there is no going back now.

The timing of the retreat was critical. I have a confession. Since signing the contract, so much fear and judgment has shown up. At times it was paralyzing. Expectations, comparison, worry that my work would not be accepted or fit in with the already "crowded field." Journaling alone at the yurt, I slowed  down enough to hear what was inside *me*, not anyone else, just my own voice. People keep telling me to read this book or that to gather ideas, but I am trying so hard to find my own voice in all this. Instead, I am working on trusting what is inside and finding my way in the dark. Patience is my mantra.

This week I had a major bump in the book road to get past, but I think it is all going to work out just fine! The roadblock and this book have provided unexpected opportunities for growth. What completely astonishes me is this—are you ready? In August, I created the card entitled, Expect the Unexpected! It is the snippet you see in the post. I created the card because I knew this was going to be a large part of this journey. Well, as if to validate that idea, the universe sent me one large surprise and an opportunity to work through some major fear and very OLD limiting beliefs.

I have been blindsided by the incredible personal process this is taking me through. My friends think this is exceptionally funny, because the book's premise is about art as process! I am living my talk and walking the path of intention every day and it is wonderful. I was able to go back to my Book of Dreams and read my June intention. In doing so, I remembered that potholes are a big part of the process. To regain my courage, I took a Dixie Chick power walk and by the time I got home, I was able to see the "gold within the lead." My intention for September is: Dance My Fear!

September Dreamer
Claudine Hellmuth

A Whole New Perspective

Imagine what creating would be like if I had total trust in my creative ability to make something just as it needed to be, without always worrying in the background if it would be good enough.

Setting My Intention

I am a big believer that thoughts become things. So when the opportunity to create an intention for a whole month came up, I jumped at the chance. At first I had no idea what my intention would be. What would I like to focus on for an entire month? Such a tricky thing! As Sheri suggested, I went through a process of sitting quietly and thinking. I settled on *trust*.

Specifically trust *in myself*, as an artist and a creative person. Trust is at the heart of so much of my daily creative worries: worry that a client won't like my work, worry that I can't create the work a client needs, worry that not enough work will come my way, worry that too much work will come my way and worry that I won't have time to do a good job. I could go on and on.

Since I could immediately think of so many examples where trust was needed in my creative life, I knew it was something to work on. Imagine what creating would be like if I had total trust in my creative ability to make something just as it needed to be, without always worrying in the background if it would be good enough. How refreshing!

Art of Intention

I started on the artwork I would use to remind me of *trust* during the month. I was drawn to the idea of eggs. Eggs are symbolic on many levels, and they are also fragile. I wanted to create a figure that would remind me of myself without using an actual photo of myself— a pseudo self-portrait of sorts. I also wanted the figure to be holding eggs in a nest—an image I think speaks to many women, including myself. The eggs would represent my ideas, my self-esteem and my trust. The artwork came pretty easily and I went with nice soothing colors, thinking this would soothe me later when I needed a trust boost.

The Experience

After creating my artwork, I expected to be reminded of my focus every time I looked at it, naïvely hoping to feel refreshed and trustful. Instead, I ended up with a *trust crisis*! I experienced a period of not trusting in my work AT ALL and hating everything I created. Focusing on trust, and why I needed to trust more, brought many things to the surface that I needed to deal with directly. I discovered that I was not trusting of my creativity and creative process! Yipes!

Once I allowed myself to have a mental temper tantrum and let the feelings of not trusting in my work run their course, my feelings slowly began to calm down. I began to look at the way I felt about my work from a whole new perspective.

For me, this was a great exercise. Even though it brought uncomfortable issues to the surface, it helped me recognize my hidden feelings, which came as a total surprise to me! I am happy to report that I am now feeling more trusting of my creative self!

October 1, 2007

Sheri's blog entry

As the days pass in this process, I see that creating this book is a journey to the depth of my soul, to find truth as it exists in my heart, without fear of the outcome. It is truly about trusting the process in the deepest of ways. I have learned so much already about showing up authentically and speaking my thoughts and beliefs from my heart.

As each artist steps into her month, we travel together into another dimension of the book. Many of the thoughts you have shared, as well as your concerns, are issues that are absolutely connected to the process of creating this book and the messages it will bring to the readers. This is exactly what I had imagined. Of course I had no idea how it would show up, it is exactly as I know it to be. After all these years I am glad that I have not lost my childlike wonderment around the work of intention. My October intention:
Dare to Be Feisty!

October Dreamer
Juliana Coles
Radiating Joy

My intention and focus this month is to create more love in my life by allowing and encouraging myself to do what I love.

October 1: Barely a week since I have returned from Greece. I am overwhelmed as I consider my life. Maybe my intention is to create love. I've worked so hard at un-love. Un-love is so strong within; where is the love? But love doesn't seem like an intention—too vague. I don't think it's right.

October 2: EnVision Intention: I've got my candle lit. What is my question to set my intention? I have so many questions, but which is the "real" one? The one at the heart of the matter, buried beneath the others? I close my eyes and ask internally, "What is at my core?" Fear, neglect, betrayal, pain, grief . . . lots of stuff. No big news—not deep enough. Eyes still closed, a voice inside says, "You let me down." When I choose someone who proves they are unworthy yet maintains my attention, I let myself down. My intention for the month is to be aware of the ways in which I let my poor baby down by allowing her to suffer. Good, but that seems like an awful lot.

October 3: I thought coming up with an intention would be easy. I can pick any ole thing and make it an intention. But if I'm going to do this and spend time on it, I want to give it my all. I'm ready for a change in my life. That's why it's difficult. I decide to look back at Sheri's suggestions for questions and light my candle again. "Where does my heart truly want to go this month?" The question doesn't elicit a response inside—no stirring. I look back at the pulsing flame of the candle. It's a Mexican "amor" candle, meant to bring love into your life—it's been sitting in front of me all along. I do not see what is in front of me. Then I ask, "What does God want me to do this month for my highest good?" I put one hand on mighty Pete, (my furry, feline companion of nineteen years) and close my eyes. The answer comes loud and clear and fast. Love. "No," I say inside me, "I can't do that." I begin to cry. So simple, so hard—I know I am on the right track. I look at the candle. Through my wet and matted eyelashes, I see a direct line of light from the candle pointing at me. Yes, but I ask again, where do I need to put my love this month? My whole life flashed before me—my job, my eating, my house, my work, my art, my relationships—where do I start? The greatest gift I can give myself is my art: That would be my greatest act of love. My intention and focus this month is to create more love in my life by allowing and encouraging myself to do what I love—what I ache for, what I long for, in healthy enjoyable ways while still getting my work done. I can also include friends, whom I would like to love more, in my plan. Each day I must do something for my artist to show her I love her, value her, respect her,

support her, encourage her, am willing to do what it takes and even make sacrifices so that she may feel my support.

October 4: When I found out what Claudine's intention had been, I was very impressed. I e-mailed her to find out how and why she chose it. I thought her intention was great and meaningful. Mine feels stupid. I need a new one. Claudine said I should call Sheri because she helped her decide by talking her through it. But I don't want to do that. I want to figure it out on my own. After all, the readers can't call her. I just feel small and very uncool.

October 5: Writing in the studio. It's warm and cozy out here. I still don't know what my intention is for the month. Time is ticking. . . I've got to get started. What am I waiting for? I want to open myself to real love, support, appreciation and relationship, but that won't come if I don't require it of those in my life, including me. I can't do this project. It's too big, too daunting—too much of my life needs attention and I can't do it all at once. I can't believe I agreed to this.

October 7: Time for another question from Sheri. If I knew I could not fail, I would . . . send my pictures to Chronicle. If I knew I could not fail, I would make a body of work. If I knew I could not fail, I would set up my online classes. If I knew I would not fail, I would hire a life coach. If I knew I would not fail—UGH. I KNOW I won't fail. What's the right prompt? If fear didn't hold me back, I would write my book. If fear didn't hold me back, I would cry. If fear didn't hold me back, I would love, smile, shed this burden that I carry so heavily and lovingly like Salome. If fear didn't hold me back, I would already have everything I want. The fear that holds me back is shame. The fear that holds me back from having everything I want is that no one loves me. The fear that holds me back from having everything I want is that I'm no good. I can't do it. I'm too slow or too stupid. I'm unhealthy. The real fear that holds me back from having the life I dream of is OVER. It's over RIGHT NOW. The real fear no longer exists. I am free to have everything I want right now. I let go of all that which no longer serves me. That was my old life. Amen.

October 10: Everything in my life seems to be about my mythology. But where is the love and happiness in this tale? Joy doesn't seem to be a part of all this in any ongoing way. Maybe it's my attitude. Look at my life: It's so great. Why am I so put out? I live my dreams. I do what I want. Why am I so angry, so agitated; what's the point? Happiness is here right now if I will have it, if I will let go of suffering and misery, my constant companions. I can do anything I want. Why aren't I? I can crack this. I just went to Greece! Where is the honor? Everything slips by in a haze of worthlessness and bad feelings.

October 12: Maybe it would be better to figure out my intention in the studio. A place where I can sit at a desk. The end of this relationship has really hurt me but made me see clearly— my final act of un-love. Life is not necessarily what I want, but it is for my highest good, and that is more than anyone could hope for. Life is complicated. That is the beauty of it. In spite of this pain, life is so beautiful, even in its most dangerous and heartbreaking moments. Grief and sadness are a natural part of the human condition. But I can't make him generous. Can I make me more generous? Could I slather that love on me?

October 14: I've been asking everyone what they think my intention should be for the month. I decide to run the issue by my Jungian Depth Psychologist. I explain the project and I tell her all my high ideas. She listens patiently. But she doesn't really respond. Not quite sure where to go next, I quietly mention the love thing. Her eyes sparkle. "Yes! That's it," she says. I say, that can't be it. She says, I know that it is. She's right. I don't know why I'm so embarrassed. Now, what am I going to do with it? What kind of piece? How do I make it tangible? It's time to prepare the studio.

October 15: Well, well. It's an odd place to find myself. I was so excited yesterday in my studio I couldn't go to bed. Time flew by. I was up 'til 1:00 a.m. I never stay up that late! Sylvia and Linda invited me over, but I didn't go. I would rather be in the studio. Who is this woman? I don't know her. I love making it real hot out there—a cozy womb. I just cleaned and played.

Life is good. Life is good. This is how I want to live every day. With joy and love for my artist because she is the core of who I am—the center of my intention. Everything else flows from that.

October 16: Everyone, all around me—all guides, help me to teach myself well. No more of this kind of treatment; it ends here. Help me see. Open my eyes. Open my ears. Open my heart to know what feels bad and to stop that bad feeling from getting out. Don't give these people one more second of my precious time. No sexy man, no tarot reader—no one. I think I hear the cranes above heading south. I have got to come up with artwork for my intention of love. I'm thinking of reworking the Sri House to make an altar, but then I like the idea of a triptych—something that opens and closes. A house of love, honor, respect and appreciation. I need to take care of me. It seems too hard, too much to do.

October 17: Today is my birthday. Terri and her husband are having me over for dinner so I won't be alone. My birthday. . . like everything else, what happened? The leaves rustling are so loud. It's shocking how they hang on in this wind. Let go. Let go. I need to do my intention project today. I thought I wanted to paint it on the wall in the dining room work area so I could see it every time I walked by, but that seemed too big, too hard, too time consuming—incredibly daunting. I don't have enough time to do something so big; I only have two weeks left. I need to feel true love in every cell; nothing else matters. I was neglected, abandoned, my health disregarded, turned into a surrogate spouse, not listened to, not taken care of, not honored or respected or appreciated. I was a nonperson. I need my love. My belief system needs my love.

October 19: Everything in my life is taking on new clarity. So I am thankful for this new information and I swear I will use it for good, and not for my undoing. Following this new perception, I suddenly draw in my journal a sketch for my intention piece. In the center is a giant heart. It feels dorky or cliché, but right. It feels good. So I go with it.

October 22: My back is stressing me out. Maybe I can write my inner self and figure out what's going on. "Hello in there. Do you know what's the matter with my back?" (Non-dominant-hand response) "I don't want to be sad anymore," it says. "I know. I feel the same way. But what does my back have to do with it?" I ask. And then it answers, "You are 'burdened' by this glorious life. You treat it like it's hard and such a drag. You get to do anything you want, when you want, yet you suffer through all the things you hate. There is no love of self or support for what you have created. It is enough. Stop seeing your life with shame and despair—always wanting to give up."

October 24: I feel like I've been enjoying my life more. It feels strange. Something feels good. I don't think I've ever said that before. It's great to hear me say that. Using the ideas and structure I used from my intention piece, I'm working on a new work for the benefit of the Harwood Art Center. I love this piece. It is rich with my symbols. And when I let go of the pressure to perform and be great, and instead allow myself to have fun, I am so happy.

October 25: I built this road, stone by stone. It is beautiful, the strange shape of it winding through time. Gather all the world beside (inside) me. My palm is still cupped, like when I was in Greece. Now it is overflowing, no longer empty waiting to be filled. My mythology: a faded story of myself and who I believed that to be. She knows deeply about fear and desire. But her agony is my triumph. I am writing a new story every day. I am changing before my very eyes. Who am I? I was a little girl. I'm growing up.

October 26: Man, the last two days have been the greatest two artist-days of all time. I can't even begin to describe how happy I've been—brimming over, I am so full. I've made a covenant: no answering the phone in the studio—no matter what. What am I going to do about this intention project? I've got to finish it! I'm supposed to be looking at it every day, not still working on it!

October 27: It's disappointing to me that I'm not working on my intention piece, but I am going out to the studio almost every day, working in my journals and on other little projects. It feels so good. This is all I've ever wanted. It's what I wish for but never do. And there is my intention piece hanging next to me. I look at it all the time and laugh. At big Jule, at baby Jule, at mighty Pete—they look so serious about taking care of me. I believe in them. I love them. I'm so glad they are there. Sometimes I find some scraps of paper and rather than put them in my journal, I put them on my piece. So, I guess I am working on it even though I don't realize it. What if I'm a famous artist already but I don't know it? Maybe people are waiting to buy my work but they can't because I won't make any and I won't put it out there.

I've been treating this intention project like any number of my perceived burdens. It's time to energize new thoughts around it—create excitement around it. After all, I'm just afraid to do what I love. And I really love this piece more than anything I have ever done. It's not for anything "important," only for me. Maybe that's why it's so hard and scary. Maybe a critic wouldn't like it. Maybe it's not big art. I don't care. The EnVision project is supporting my future, my artist, my path. It is helping me like Papolo in the Ecuadorian jungle, slicing a path for us with his machete. He made it look so easy.

October 28: I'm realizing art takes a long time. I always want to hurry it up, take the bread out of the oven before it is ready. This is a big project, both literally and symbolically, and I mistakenly thought I could whip it out in a few hours or maybe a weekend.

October 29: My project is not done. I haven't worked on it as much as I would have liked; there is always something to do, like the project for the Harwood. But I guess the real accomplishment is that I've been out in the studio practically every day. Maybe the project is not the thing, but the energy around it. I don't want to hurry it. I keep feeling pressure and failure. Leave me alone. I'm doing fine. Honestly, I am so proud of myself. I am astounded at what I'm doing. My studio life is affecting my whole being. Work is still getting done and no one has died or yelled at me. Now I know why the Minotaur was so submissive and accepting of his death. My monsters bow their heads; they know it is time to go. It is right. It is safe to let them go.

October 30: I'm so worried about my piece for the Harwood Art Center. And like my EnVision project, I have so much pressure around it. I haven't been in an Albuquerque exhibit for years. It's like my debut and I want to do something great, but I don't know who I am as an artist anymore. I have changed so much, what does my work look like now? Maybe I'm a sculptor, maybe a photographer. And what if my work is substandard from not working all this time? People might laugh. They may not like it. They may not like me. It's going to be an anonymous showing for the fundraiser; no one will even know it is my piece. I feel disguised and safe. I made something I love. It seems very different for me. I am worried it is weird. What if no one buys it? I love it, so I will buy it if no one else does.

October 31: It is safe to create a body of work. It is safe to create a body of work. It is safe to create a body of work. It is valuable for me to create a body of work. It is loving for me to create a body of work. It is beautiful for me to create a body of work. It is safe for me to work on my intention. My art matters. It is safe for my art to matter. It is safe for me to create art that matters. My art matters. My voice matters. My visual journals matter. All that I create has worth and value. I matter, therefore I can create. I matter, so it is from this safe protected place I create a body of work. My studio is a safe, magical space to create art that is full of my love. My creations matter, my world matters. This is between me and God and Pete. No one else gets to decide. I create because I am a creator. I create because it is a gift from God. To deny myself is to deny God and the world. It's the end of the month. I haven't finished. I'm going to let that be okay. I feel like this project is going to take me a very long time to finish. I'm going to let this child continue to grow. I'll be supportive. I'll love her. I'll let her be. I won't strong-arm her into something I need her to be when she's not ready. I'll tell her she's beautiful, rather than hurt her feelings with criticisms and judgments. I'll protect her from those who won't understand her. I need to get out to the studio.

⑤ Layering with a Transparency

Artist Juliana Coles is known for her Extreme Journaling techniques. Here, I am recreating one technique she uses—how to use a transparency sheet to add layers to your work.

What You Need

pre-painted background in your Book of Dreams Journal

decorative papers

acrylic paints

small brush

gel medium

photo-editing software

digital, high-contrast image

transparency sheet for your printer

rub-on words

Titan Buff acrylic paint (Golden)

packing tape

① Begin by creating a random background in your journal, with layers of decorative papers and any painting that you like. Seal the page with a coat of gel medium and set it aside to dry. Open your photo-editing software and open up an image that has a good range of contrast, such as a building or iron gate. This should be symbolic to you in some way. Go to Edit/Adjustment/Desaturate. You should now have a black and white image. Now go to adjust the contrast and up the contrast. Print out your image onto a transparency.

② Select some words or phrases from a rub-on sheet and apply them to the front of the transparency, in a clear or relatively blank area.

3 Peel up the sheet to reveal the rub-on, then turn the transparency over. Apply Titan Buff to the area behind the transferred word.

4 Secure the transparency to the journal page with a rough-cut piece of packing tape.

5 One fun element of the transparency is to be able to fold it back to reveal a "secret" behind it. Here, I want to add a rub-on word behind the word added to the transparency. First add a swash of Titan Buff over the page where the rub-on will go.

6 Let the paint dry, then add the rub-ons.

7 Dab paint roughly around the perimeter of the front of the transparency and let it dry. Doodle or write on top of the paint for added depth.

Sheri's blog entry

Yesterday, I shared September's art-of-intention piece with a friend; the title is Dance Your Fear. My friend asked which part of the painting I was most attracted to. I told her it was the wings I was most drawn to and said, "Although they are translucent and golden, they feel strong enough to carry me through this process."

Then . . .magic occurs. Today while on my morning hike, we looked down to see a dragonfly, nearly translucent, and the color of the brown/red earth. I picked it up; it was still moving, barely alive. I set the dragonfly down on a stone and, reminding her she could fly, said a little prayer for her journey. When I returned two hours later, she was gone. I thought she had flown away and I felt a sense of joy at her release. Out of the corner of my eye, I saw some movement in the dirt below and there she was. About twenty ants were carrying her away and her legs were still moving! I was horrified at the sight and with a maternal instinct I could not understand, I worked at gently freeing her body from the ants. When she was free, I picked her up and carried her home, her tiny body safeguarded within the enclosure of my hands.

My friend told me it was just body memory that was making her legs move, yet something inside me needed to protect her. And as we got to the car I realized what it was. Her translucent wings were reminiscent of my own—the wings that I painted in this month's intention, yet the dragonfly no longer had the strength to protect herself or fly away. The dragonfly is now on my studio windowsill with a collection of other natural elements I have found along the way. A reminder of the discovery I made last month about fear, authenticity and faith.

I also took another bold step. I shared some of the first art pieces with SWIRL, a writers group I was blessed to be invited to join a few years ago. I still feel too vulnerable to share my writing with anyone, but I wanted to get some feedback on the few pieces I have created for the deck so far. As they were writing notes about the images, I looked out the window and noticed the kids doing something on the lawn across the street. In the next moment, I was called back to the group to hear their thoughts.

When we were finished, the group asked me what next month's intention was. I pulled out my Book of Dreams and showed it to them.

At two in the morning, my unconscious woke me out of a deep sleep and I realized what I had seen across the street. The kids had set up a line and were literally trying to balance on it and use it as a tightrope! And yes, the sketch I had shown them was about finding balance! Balance between the book, my clients and my life. My September intention: Finding Balance!

November Dreamer
Deborah Koff-Chapin
Drawing Out the Soul

My core desire is to find the place of creative resonance in my day-to-day life.

I am in my studio, in the moment of stepping over the threshold of resistance to writing. I write for work, a different stream of my soul. I am not a journal writer or poet. This realm sits in potential yet does not call to me of resonance, beauty or life. The images do; the music does. So here is my task: to find a way to fill these pages with words about a process that I am supposed to be engaging in. Arriving at an intention, creating a single image that embodies that intention, meditating upon that image for a month and seeing what arises in life in response to this focus.

To begin with, the month I chose was the busiest travel month I have ever had. My first thought was that this project would help me keep a creative focus during that time. Thank goodness I did not depend upon that possibility and instead decided to begin in the previous month.

Setting My Intention

What could my intention be? My core desire is to find the place of creative resonance in my day-to-day life. Though my life is supposedly about that, most of my days are spent in the office taking care of the multitude of details that revolve

around my work with Touch Drawing. On a deep level, I have felt distant from my creative core—my inspiration. I have become tired of hearing myself talk or even think about this. Tired of it as an issue—just wanting to get beyond it. Before creating my image, I set my intention with these words:

I want to bring myself more fully into my potential self.
What is really important for me?
What is really important for the planet?
Are they the same?
Balance my days; spend time in the studio each day; use my time clearly to go deeper into the potential of my creative life.
Break out of habitual day-to-day time wasters.
Commit to the soul life.
Reach in and under,
Find the joy of the creative life once again.
Feel engaged in a deeper emergence.
Be engaged in a deeper emergence.
Feel the life behind the creation.
Feel called to create once again.

The Art of Intention

I will create an image that carries this intention. But I cannot create a singular image. In my process, Touch Drawing, a series of spontaneous images can emerge in one sitting through the touch of fingertips on paper. I dab some paint on my drawing board, roll it smooth and place

a sheet of paper on top. Then I give my attention to how I feel in this moment—a raw, real place. I then move my fingertips on the paper, tracing my inner sensations. I pull the paper off the board, glance at my first drawing and then I lay it aside and bring my awareness to how I feel once again. I begin to aim my psyche in the direction of my intention. Can I begin to imagine what it would feel like to live in this creative, resonant state? I cannot just create a "picture" from an idea of it. I must embody it, to draw it there. I stay with this process, doing one drawing after another until I have a sense of completion. The following words describe something of the process I moved through as the series emerged.

1. I sit at my drawing board. The paint is rolled out. The paper is placed upon it. I am ready to begin. I am just here. No particular feeling. I close my eyes and turn inward. How do I feel in this moment? My fingertips trace the simple forms onto the page—closed eyes, nose, mouth, periphery of my head. Around and around in darkness. I pull this drawing off the board, glance at the simple inky face and lay it aside. Roll the paint smooth and place another sheet of paper onto the board.

2. I reach inward with my feeling body. Calling for that ephemeral thing called inspiration. Arms reach inward as open wings. Free of form, free of fingers, opening to the unknown, to the emptiness. I move the paper and rub over that winged place, multiple wings lifting into the unknown.

3. Oh, mucky creative chaos. Tear it open. Spin it around. Nowhere, nothing, weighted with the spinning into nowhere. Nowhere. Just be here in this, in my body

and out. Open the chakra of expression. It doesn't matter anyway. Just another piece of paper, another rush into the moment.

4. Ah, a flame; something ignites in the belly. Still of nothing, but with warmth, a burning. It rises through the heart, rises through the neck. Rises to the tip of my tongue—just beginning. But alit? My face is circled in another light. They meet. They touch. They overlap. They begin.

5. Ah, yes; a resonance. The flaming emptiness moves through my being and alights upon my fingers, firing into the world from within the darkness of my unknowing heart. But emerged, aflame, incarnate. The unlit light from another realm resonates as it flows from beyond to within, to harmonize with the burning earth in flaming song. (This is the image that crystallizes my intention.)

6. Inward once again to feel the resonance as it reverberates within. It swirls and turns and yet I am still and dark and unknowing within it. Rest in being. No need for an image.

7. Eyes glow in fiery light, yet I am deep in the darkest unknowing. I think I would like to delete this drawing and its text.

8. This drawing had been missing its writing. Here it is: Opening my eyes to the vibrancy of being; opening my being to vibrance.

9. I come into being and essence. Memories reside within, yet I flow only in the moment. The future is reflected in unseen eyes. Only one eye. Only eternity. Nothing new. Nothing to create. Only being here, again and again and again and again in the eternal dance of the heart.

EnVision Reflections

As Sheri suggested, I hung the images on my studio wall and tried reflecting on them each day. Many days—even in my month at home—were so full of the busyness of life that I didn't even have the pull of stepping into the studio to gaze upon them. I did when I could. I walked in for a moment to reflect upon her and hope she entered my being. I made plane reservations, ordered materials, booked hotels, arranged visits, located directions—a jigsaw puzzle of airports and art supplies and packing and shipping and arranging. . . But during all of that, I internalized the image enough to know that at least it did exist in my psyche.

I didn't much like the drawings. They seemed a bit flat, a bit obvious. They sagged on the walls of my psyche. I had done my assignment, but had I really done anything? It would just have to wait while I went on with weeks of movement from world to world: workshops, conferences, family visits. Literal, real stuff. Moments of magic, moments of music and many, many airports.

Finally home in mid-December, all I wanted to do was clean. Even though it's dirty again in a day, I cleaned: cabinets, floors, candleholders. I resisted writing. The words felt like empty anti-inspirations. Not what brings the light to my soul. Yet a part of my intention, my longing for more creative resonance, is to sing more. My usual being wordless flows of the moment. Yet there is a wondering, a maybe longing, to find the well of words that form within the sound. At the same time a sense that those words are so easily stupidly superficial. I feel that wordless resistance to words once again.

I decide that I will at least spend time with the drawings through coloring them.

Wonderful, mindless, time moving among their lines, and forms with wet flowing layers and fine forming refinements. Calling the images more fully into being. And being with them. Maybe something will become more real. This is my honest way of being with them. I spend hours—a week, maybe two—with this set of drawings as my focus—coaxing them into fuller presence with layers of more. Is this less honest than the first raw drawings? Is this honest or just an attempt to turn them into "art"?

I am so close to being done and feel the deadline approaching. I must find those 2,500 little ethereal things called words. I don't want the coloring to end.

The Convergence

After a year of considering, I have my first voice lesson with a woman who can help me find my words in song. We are in my studio. I pull out the drawings to reflect my longing to reignite the creative flame. I realize that this is a convergent moment. The day I can no longer put off finding words for this project is the day I no longer put off finding words for my song. Maybe something real is converging here.

So, I have begun to write. And this is what I wrote. What is my word count? Including this question, 1,545.

Field Note

To order a CD-ROM that will guide you through this experience, visit Deborah's Web site, listed in the Resource section, page 139.

6 Painting by Touch

In this step-out I'm demonstrating Deborah's Touch Drawing technique. Remember, Deborah has been creating Touch Drawings for a very long time and creates phenomenal and detailed intuitive paintings. Deborah reminds us, "This is NOT about making a pretty painting. It is about tapping into your inner awareness and intuition."

What You Need

water-soluble oil paint

Touch Painting board (see Resources, page 139, for Deborah's Web site)

brayer

newsprint or tracing paper

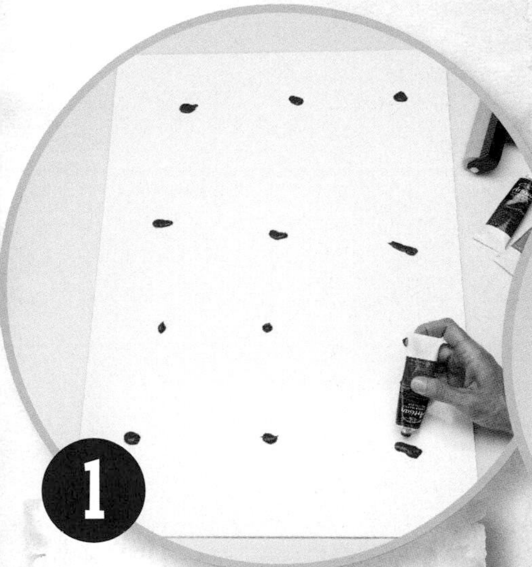

1

Squeeze several dollops of paint onto the surface of the board. It is best to start with one color.

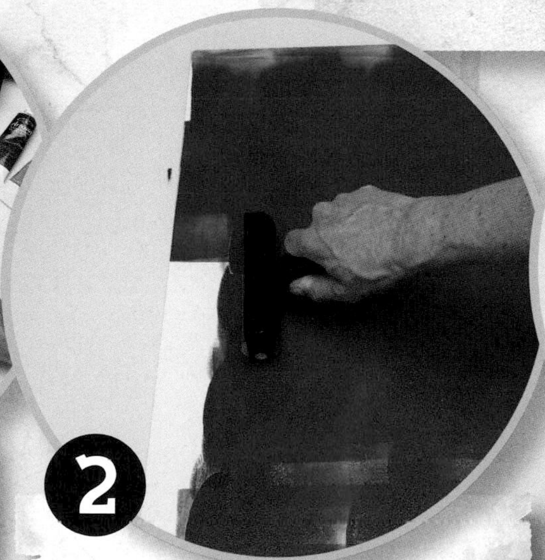

2

Use a brayer to spread the paint and roll it out smoothly over the entire surface of the board.

3

Put a piece of newsprint over the paint and use both hands to create your painting. Do this by touching the paper with your fingernails, fingertips and palms. Try using both hands some of the time. Try drawing with your eyes closed. Let your hands dance on the page. Become aware of body sensations and trace them on the paper. They might be abstract patterns or images.

4

Gently peel back the paper to reveal the print. Roll the board smooth and begin another painting with a new piece of paper. (Add paint after a few drawings.) Draw whatever you feel in the moment. When you are finished drawing, roll the paint smooth and let it dry.

Letter to fellow dreamers

I am moving into December with my intention of "Letting Go of the Reins." The image is complete. It literally poured out of me. It was as if everything that transpired in November allowed me to see what was truly important, and for that I am really grateful. Ego and fear are now tucked away in a box on the shelf. I am ready. I am ready to let go of my fears about my art and how, or if, it will be "accepted." Ready to let go of my writing and the question of whether I have anything poignant to say. I am ready to let go and believe that I am birthing this book to the best of my ability.

I believe in my heart and soul we are bringing something to the world that has value and I hope will make a difference in people's lives. Each of you is an example of what is truly possible, when we believe. That is all that matters to me in the end.

If the ideas we are sharing with the readers touch one person in a way that changes their life, then it will all have been worth the journey.

I am so grateful that you are in this with me. I feel your hands on my back. By joining me, you have given me the greatest gifts, those of your time and your incredible talent.

13 20 27

12 # December Dreamer
Anahata Katkin
18 25
Moving On

11

10 17 24 31

I find that if I can just let the intention go, it will show me something in the end.

I find that thinking about the changes I want to make can be powerful, and writing it can be even more so. But when intention is set to the tune of the arts, there is something that occurs that is so dynamic it cannot be dismissed.

I have turned to my creativity in times of desperation and in times of joy. I have taken refuge in the arts after years without making a single thing, and, of course, in times of great proliferation. In my life, the effects of the creative process are threefold: It has the power to relieve my tension and stress. It has the power to inform me about my current, past and future circumstances. (Perspectives are often revealed in the artwork itself.) And, miraculously, in art exploration, an insight about my dilemma is often revealed.

By doing artwork, I feel I am able to access a more trusting and intuitive side of myself. The idea of clicking into the creative space means tuning out the world and inviting a bit of grace inside. Still, I have to remind myself to apply the creative process to solutions in my life. Just like eating poorly and not exercising, I can slip into old habits of creating and not use it as the powerful tool for change that it truly is.

When I was younger I was full of hope and an abundance of optimism. I have always felt cared for by life and trusted that things would only get better and better. I imagined myself becoming the woman of my own fantasy: full of wisdom and strength, full of charisma and positivity. Slowly life has taken bites out of that fresh perspective and it often seems I am running on empty, wondering where my zest for life has gone and how it can be that I am not fulfilled, even though my life is full of blessings.

I live a wonderful life that includes travel, a full-time arts career, enough money to pay the bills and a beautiful son. There is nothing that is "wrong" so to speak. But life hasn't been feeling as good as it should. I've been achieving so many dreams, and still I feel sleepy for life.

When I originally reached for a topic for the exercises in this book, it was because it felt digestible to me on a public level. I wanted to choose something that wasn't too revealing. As the artwork itself unfolded—as it always does—the truth (the elephant in the living room) could not be avoided. The artwork revealed to me that despite my efforts to remain lighthearted, I wouldn't be able to express anything other than the truth. The artwork has the last word and tells the real story, every time.

That's what is so amazing to me about the creative process. It is very difficult to

hide. You can see a person in their creative layers. You can identify an overall personality and style, and you can also identify a mood and a chapter someone is in just by looking at what they express. The artwork isn't always representing the totality of a person, but it signals what is important to them in the moment.

At one point, my life did the falling apart act. I rebuilt my perspective through creative determination and entrepreneurial business. I became obsessed with my work and decided to let myself fall by the wayside until I could pick up the pieces. It worked.

But lately, more than ever, I can feel the bites that grief took out of my life along the way. Now I search my face for signs of the real me. I am looking more and more for the parts of myself that I've neglected.

When my first vision of family fell apart, it created a rift in my beliefs. It affected my mentality on every level. And now, many years later, I see that I have been cooking "resentment stew" for far too long.

I am the kind of person who is always trying to better my thinking and encourage my own well-being. But somehow I have been able to avoid the real work of moving on. I used to wonder how women got those furrowed brows and stern faces. How could they not change their discomfort and the clear signs of years of self sabotage? I suppose that hard lesson has been in my court, and quietly my shadow of disappointment and confusion has crept in on me and reminded me of all those generations before me.

All these years later, as I am trying to change my body and my health, I can feel the undertow of the past. Somehow I must find a way to truly let go of resentments and all the negative momentum that has cut me off from my vitality. I know it and I feel it.

One of the key tools for me lately has been the images reflected to me in my artwork. The faces are like friends who need a cup of tea and a good walk—faces with stories and worries. And I like them, like good friends. I appreciate their strengths and their beauty. I can see what they cannot. And that is the advantage I don't always have when I look in the mirror. My artwork helps me to gain insights about what it is I need and where my good qualities are latent or deliberate.

When I was in college I painted and sculpted mostly nude women. They were always arching, dancing and playing, and they were vivid. They were expressive and bright but very overdramatic. They weren't my best creative works, but they indicated me as a person.

Today the artwork shown is a piece that is clearly a figure like so many faces I see in my artwork staring back at me over many years—like my own image, a stern and powerful figure with determination in her eyes. She intrigues me and she is alive, but she's lacking joy and playfulness. When I looked at this image, I noticed one of the things that made me buy the original antique photo in the first place. It was the big ribbon around the woman's neck. She had that dress closed up to her chin and tied off with that big bow, which looked so lovely at first.

But now that I am finished, I see something different. She looks controlled to me and doesn't look free to play and dance. She almost looks like an empress. And to me, that means responsibility, duty and obligation. She's literally "buttoned up."

And what I see in her eyes is the thing I want to change most. *Resentment.* No matter how I try to improve my life, nothing is going to feel different until I address the bitterness that has kept me from feeling a sense of sustained contentment.

All in all, I like this image, though. I have always loved contrast, and I need a bit of grit in my artwork. It will always be part of my style. But I have to be honest and see what I see there, too.

I always create primarily on impulse, starting with a favorite photo or simply working with a background to get the ball rolling. Then I react to one thing at a time. Never planning or thinking too far ahead, I try and let the artwork emerge organically. If I don't worry too much about the outcome, I can surprise myself.

When I am doing a project with an intention in mind, I specifically set that intention and then release it, just like a prayer. I don't look for symbols or perfect elements to represent my intention. I find that if I can just let the intention go, it will show me something in the end. That said, the result can often be shocking.

I once made a piece while I was under a great deal of stress and was really angry. I was determined to sort of let it out. I chopped up paper bits and worked away at it very quickly. I was going to have my grumpy little tantrum project soon enough. But by the end I had calmed my anger and gotten into the delicious art trance after about an hour. What emerged that day was in fact a very delightful and inspiring piece full of pinks and white. She seemed peaceful and relaxed. It was not at all what I had set out to create. She

just emerged. And when she was done I felt better and had actually turned a new leaf that day.

The same can be true when we set out with positive intentions to create some beautiful vision of what we hope to become. Sometimes where we are right now shows up first. I like to look at the artwork and be satisfied with both a job well done and with the insights from the artwork itself. I don't want to look at any creation and judge it, but rather enjoy the information and the addition to my fantasy cast of inner characters.

I am comforted by my piece, and I see the plant forms on either side of her. I like to imagine that she is holding them. To me they sort of represent olive branches, which signify peace (often after a time of challenge). And those branches are actually made of vintage road maps. I see this character as an aspect of myself that is asking me to let go and to leave her behind. Like a master releasing a wild bird, she calls me forward and tells me it's OK to see her fade away.

She says to me that there will be peace in letting go. Peace in moving on. It's time to renovate my smile and my ability to feel hopeful again. It's time to build a new vision of family and a new vision of self. And she will be here to remind me not to look back.

MILE MARKER 7 Altering a Magazine Image

Photos can be easily integrated into any background, or a background can be built around an image. I recommend doing a little of both. Create a background using paint, collage or drawing. Add in your photo or focal image. Then find ways to embellish the new photo while also adding new doodles to your background. This will give your project lots of depth and make your artwork look intentional without ever having to plan ahead.

What You Need

paper prepared with paint or collage

computer scanner

digital images of figures, 2

scissors

glue

pre-painted background in your Book of Dreams or other paper

gel pen

Titan Buff acrylic paint (Golden)

1 Create a background using paint or collage. Scan a figure, print it out and cut it out with scissors. Adhere the cutout figure to your painted background.

2 Glue the figure and painted background onto a pre-painted page in your journal or onto a new piece of paper.

3 Scan a different figure, in a pose that you like, print it out and cut it out with scissors. Adhere that over the figure on the background.

4 Use a gel pen to add details to the figure and the surrounding background. Here I created shutters to give the illusion of a window. I added Titan Buff to separate them from the background. Let dry.

Sheri's blog entry

Today is my birthday and I have a longtime ritual that I did not want to alter. Since my birthday is so close to the New Year, I make my birthday a special time for reflection and intention setting and today I took some time to do just that. I created a double-page spread in my Book of Dreams. The first page celebrates the past year, and the second depicts my intentions and hopes for the year ahead.

The piece I chose to work with in my Book of Dreams is a photo of me in my grandmother's backyard. In the image, I am wearing a sailor's outfit and my pose is that of a curtsy, complete with skinned knee! I actually did not notice the skinned knee until a friend pointed it out to me. Her observation made me smile, as I think this photo might sum up the person I feel I have become—and, perhaps, always was.

As I look at the image of myself as a sweet and hopeful three-year-old, I realize it has been a long journey to this moment. Her path has certainly not been a linear one, and oftentimes the road has been rocky, but she is a lot stronger and more courageous for it. As I look in her eyes, I feel closer to her today than perhaps at any other moment in my life. We have traveled these roads of life together to find a sense of peace, joy and content-ment and a newfound sense of hope and gratitude. I wrote in my high school twentieth-reunion booklet, "Life's a journey and I feel like I found my path." My intention this month: Create a New Story.

January Dreamer
Mary Beth Shaw
The Clarity Cave

Finally, I knew what I would envision for myself. A path to clarity.

When Sheri asked me to become involved with her book, I instantly knew I wanted to do the month of January because it is always a time of renewal for me. Typically I hibernate after the holidays and review my goals from the prior year, then establish new goals. I thought working Sheri's process into my usual routine of self work would be a no-brainer. I mean, duh, I do this stuff already. Geez, if only I had known that I would end 2007 spinning like a top. . . but, I am jumping ahead of myself.

Although 2007 was certainly successful, it was a whirlwind of tornadic force, and I ended the year *exhausted* having participated in nineteen art fairs and gallery exhibits. I was clearly pleased with my artistic achievements, but I also felt I had missed quality time with family and friends because I was so frequently out of town selling my art. Combine my desire for balance with the woes of the economy and increasing travel expenses, and you might guess this biz-minded artist knew that she would have to rethink her strategy.

So, bright-eyed and bushy-tailed, as my mom would say, I started January first (could I be any more of a teacher's pet/dork?) by puzzling over a solution, a way for me to regroup yet still support myself as a successful professional. Honestly, I thought I would buzz right through this process with little effort. I imagined deeply moving internal time

followed by some sort of cathartic experience and then the big *aha* moment that would transform my life forever.

My usual routine includes regular meditation, but for some reason I had a horrible time quieting the inner voices that first day. My mind was all over the place and I kept coming back to tree branches. I imagined my art business as having multiple paths, all open to journey. I saw myself wandering aimlessly, trying one path after another, being slapped by branches, living Mary Oliver's poem *The Journey*. In my mind, the limbs were the paths but were simultaneously blocking the paths; they seemed to be telling me to branch out. I made a journal entry about the process but couldn't find any peace with my thoughts.

Two days later I tried again. Same thing, there was so much noisy static in my brain it was unbelievable, and I knew I was trying too hard—like when someone tells you to not think about the color blue but of course that is all you can think about. I ended up just playing in my journal for a while, doing freeform doodling and stream-of-consciousness writing. I tried again and again over the next few days (because I am stubbornly persistent) and got off on a wild tangent about a new body of work I wanted to make (and have since started).

Finally, my fifth session, I hit on something that seemed big. Now mind you, I have always been obsessed with text and I use it frequently in my work. In my meditation, still unable to let my mind go blank, I saw letters, random fonts and text dancing. The

The Cave In

Your Fortune-Teller

letter P was prominent. I could not stop thinking about the word *percolate*. Yes, as in coffee. I realized that this is what I was doing. I was percolating and trying to distill my thoughts down into some cohesive direction. I also got to thinking about P's in general, about my *p*urpose and my *p*assion for *p*aint. I concluded that my *p*ath for January was to percolate.

But alas, about a week later, I meditated again, going to a very quiet place in my mind where I finally found the bliss of peace. I made a follow-up journal entry about boxes, perhaps spawned by a friend of mine who had decided to make her year's theme Out of the Box. Truly, I mused, perhaps my theme should be Get Back in Your Box. I mean, seriously, sometimes I am sooooo all over the place; I hardly need more encouragement.

Days later, after another meditation session, I journaled about the letter C, and that is when it hit me like a ton of bricks. The month was about *clarity*. I wanted and needed to gain clarity into my situation and to C or see or envision my future in its entire splendor. Obviously, percolating was my path. Finally, I knew what I would envision for myself—a path to clarity.

The following weeks were an excavation of sorts as I delved into my mind and played around with different ideas. At one point I had so many ideas flitting around—butterflies I could not herd—I did what I call a mind dump and just wrote down everything that I could think of in a very aimless fashion. Later, I organized these thoughts into a mind map that I would subsequently use as a more efficient guide.

My collage painting, *The Clarity Cave,* was largely intuitive. I started working in a frenzy of activity and suddenly it was there before me, one of those glorious times when I go so deep into my process that I enter a zone where I lose track of time and forget to eat and pee. That is how this painting happened. As I studied it day after day, its meaning became clear.

The Clarity Cave basically illustrates what I want to unfold during the coming year. The symbolic elements consist of a topographical map and hand-painted tissue paper that form the first layer and set the framework for a complicated journey of textured layers. The image of the girl is me as a child. I altered it first, using digital-imaging software, to appear as an X-ray or negative image, a mysterious, more internalized version of myself. *The Fortune Teller* is a vintage image I selected for her stern yet spectral appearance. I imagined her as my guide. The wheel of letters was perfect, as were the snippets of film that represent a kind of "this is your life" piece. And the fish—oh my darling little fish image—she represents me, finally coming up for air.

So, now that all is said and done, I guess I did have my internal time after all, and it did lead to a cathartic transformational moment. Ironically, when I pulled a card from the deck (which was sent around the group of dreamers, along with the Awakenings Round-Robin Journal), I pulled a card that spoke about growth—*ha!* What have I been doing but growing and growing? I've not only achieved personal growth as an artist, but growth toward a lifestyle that will be better managed and supported by alternative paths. In addition, growth as a human being because I finally admitted I require more time for family and for myself. Do I have complete clarity? Well, not complete, but I think I'd need a crystal ball for that! I do know that I have focus, a plan, and I know that it is working.

During the month, I achieved one of my longtime dreams to conduct a Studio Workshop (actually I had two of them, groups of four people each that came to my studio for an all-day painting workshop). It was largely process-oriented, chock-full of techniques, and I loved the intimacy of teaching such small groups. It was perfect and exactly what I had envisioned. Other goals are falling into place as well. I envisioned selectively decreasing my art fair schedule during the 2008 season, and so far I am right on track with one top show scheduled for each month—April, May, June and July. Once again, exactly what I had envisioned. And finally, I wholesaled some smaller works and reproductions to a gallery that will host a show of my originals later this year. Yes, exactly what I had envisioned.

It was an amazing month and a powerful way to start the year!

⑧ Creating Texture on a Painting

Using Claybord as a stubstrate is an easy way to get instant texture into your mixed-media pieces. Its uses are varied and the results can add surprising and unexpected elements to your artwork. Here, I'm trying out some of artist Mary Beth Shaw's secrets for texture like those she used for the piece, *The Clarity Cave*.

What You Need

Claybord (Ampersand)

acrylic paint

matte gel medium

paintbrush

colored pencil

carving tools

Dremel tool

wire brush

sandpaper

1 Paint over the Claybord with thin layers of paint mixed with gel medium. There shouldn't be a lot of paint on your brush. Here, I made a layer of green-gold mixed with yellow, then added a layer of ultramarine blue over the top.

2 Let the paint dry, then use a colored pencil to sketch out your desired composition. Here, I'm using a white pencil so it shows up against the blue. If you make a mark you don't want, it's usually easy enough to just rub it out.

3 Use a fine carving tool to scrape outlines of the lines you've drawn.

4 Use the Dremel tool to scratch texture into some of the shapes, like these flower petals.

5 Use a wire brush to create cross-hatching texture.

6 Use sandpaper to soften areas and add subtle distressing.

Letter to fellow dreamers

Dear Dreamers,

Drum rolls please. . . I have a very important February announcement! I received an e-mail on January 31 and we now have an official title! The book has been named: *Creative Awakenings: Envisioning the Life of Your Dreams Through Art.*

I have a confession to make. When I signed the contract, I was not aware that the publisher would name my book. Yes, I was a newbie. I have been so attached to my submitted title, Twelve Months of Dreams, it has been extremely difficult to let go. Attachment, letting go, picking my battles. . . All of these have been a part of my mantra from the start, so it is a very good thing I created the Letting Go of the Reins card back in December.

As you all know, the first selected title was so out of sync with my philosophy and beliefs that I had a bit of a tantrum! I admit it, but really, this is like carrying your first child to term and then turning it over to someone else to name. After hearing your feedback—a wonderful validation—I knew I was not alone, and that gave me the courage to assert myself and share again the words I believed were very important to the book concept. My wonderful editor listened and heard our plea and then came up with the one we now have. In the end, although this was not my choice, it does, as Tonia reminded me, have three words that were very important to me: creative, envision and dreams. Tonia—ever my cheerleader—told me she hoped that I would "grow to love it."

It was time to take Tonia's helpful advice, so I decided to try it on. This way I could really envision it (no pun intended). I made printouts of the title and hung it where I would see it each day. I started sharing the title with friends and family, and today I decided I would create a page in my Book of Dreams to give the title roots to grow.

And here is what happened: It has been almost a week, and I have in fact grown to love it. Interestingly, my first newsletter series was titled Creative Transformations. My newsletter title has since been changed, but I realized this is not far from that and wonder if this is not some kind of sign? I have started to share the new title with people I meet in town and with clients and students. I am hearing responses like, "Oh—that feels very much like what you do," which has helped me to now Believe It!

Once I was able to look at this from all angles—and get out of my own way (i.e., let go of the reins)—I was able to embrace it and see how sometimes my need to control things might not always serve me in the best way.

It is time for some much-needed rest and restoration. This month's intention is to take a Gypsy Spirit Day!

Thank you for your love and support during this process. I still pinch myself and know how blessed I am to have you all in this Dreamer's Circle.

February Dreamer
Suzanne Simanaitis

Addition by Subtraction: An Artist Finds Herself Amidst the Clutter

That's why it's so sad and so difficult to get rid of all this stuff. It feels like I'm abandoning the dreams that go with it.

February 1: Even my dearest friends and family are rarely invited to my house, because it is always such a mess—I mean chaos. Plump tote bags crammed into closets. Cabinet doors that don't latch because there's so much stuff wedged inside. Baskets of boxes. Bins of tins. After I die, the hazmat crew will be called to my house to remove stacks of potentially moldy 1950s *Vogue* magazines. I used to consider my pack rat tendencies benign, even noble. Hey, I'm frugal. As an artist who works in mixed media, I can lump just about anything—possibly everything—under the heading of "potential art supply."

At some point, my stuff took charge and I began a long retreat into smaller workspaces, smaller projects, smaller dreams. Today, I'm unable to find enough room to work on my art. If I do clear some space, I become paralyzed by the variety of materials available. When I'm able to decide, I'm unable to locate the stuff I want. If I can gather the desired materials, I can't concentrate on the creative process because I feel guilty about the mess. It's a constant cycle of disappointment.

My intention is to reclaim some territory and clear the clutter that is dragging me down. A shrink would say I must be "getting" something from the stuff. I need to figure out what that payoff is and strike a new bargain with myself, because this is no way to live.

February 2: Hmm, nice pep talk, but it's day two and I haven't yet tossed a single thing. I sit on the sofa with a roll of trash bags on one side, a "giveaway" box on the other. I've surrounded myself with precarious piles of stuff and an impressive quantity of big, empty rubber bins. They won't stay empty for long, and after a while they don't seem quite so big anymore. I had a vision of carefully sorted inspirational art supplies stacked neatly in a row, but I am amazed and overwhelmed by the enormous volume of crap I drag out of closets and drawers. I take a deep breath. The sorting begins.

February 4: I bought my house just before the Los Angeles real estate market went crazy and even "starter" homes like mine were suddenly out of reach. It's tiny but it's all mine. I had such exciting dreams for each room . . . but one unexpected circumstance after another kept me from putting plans into motion. Now, six years later, I am miserable where I should be happy. Not only am I drowning in clutter, but I am also disappointed, even embarrassed, that in no way does my home reflect my true self.

Wait, let me rephrase that, because I'm beginning to get some clarity here. This mess does reflect the current state of my mind, I now admit. I see that in addition to dejunking my environment, I must declutter my brain and ditch the thought patterns that have created this situation.

I read somewhere that putting junk into new containers to save it for "someday" is like covering a tumor with a Band-Aid. Organizing clutter imparts make-believe

meaning to it and perpetuates the myth that all the imagined "somedays" are achievable. If I am truly honest, I don't even want many of these imagined "somedays" anymore. Deletion, not organization, is going to be key in finding my way out of this mess.

February 6: Surely I do not own fifty-seven quarts of wool roving. . . . Well, yes I do—three big, stuffed, plastic bins. I remember buying the first of it a decade ago, inspired by a felting workshop. Yet most of that wool stayed right here in these bins.

This hoarding is symptomatic of a failure to live in the present. I saw, I desired, I bought. That felt gratifying. But I didn't follow through on the vision; now I barely recall that beautiful object I so fervently wished to create.

Here's why it's so difficult to get rid of all this stuff: It feels like I'm abandoning the dreams that go with it.

I stubbornly cram all fifty-seven quarts of roving into three bins, still unwilling to admit defeat. I shove everything off the sofa and curl up for a good, long cry. A nap is impossible, thanks to the "giveaway" box that is poking me in the back, as if to say, "Hey! I'm still here to help." Maybe tomorrow I'll listen.

February 9: I chip away at the mountain of stuff, resisting, resenting and failing to let go of much, but finally I claim small victories, like liberating the printed tins that represented me, circa 2002, stuffed in a closet and gathering dust. One small breakthrough leads to another, and I find myself ready to release a bunch of tools so they will relinquish their hold on me. But. . . .this stuff is too "good" to throw away; it's all too specialized to send to a thrift shop . . . so, do I hold an artsy yard sale? Even having "let it go" in my mind, I'm still not sure where to send it, and until it's out of my house, it's not really gone. These things may have a certain value, but they are costing me.

February 11: I tell myself to be patient. I wish I could sweep the clutter into the trash in one grand gesture, but I can't, and I'm not going to beat myself up over it. The favorite fabrics, the cherished seashells, the fascinating vintage travel diary. . . I want to keep it all and wait for the perfect application to reveal itself to me.

And there's the real problem that lurks beneath all this hoarded stuff: perfectionism. Not only do I hesitate to toss stuff, I hesitate to use it because I fear wasting it. I am afraid I'll be unable to create the desired outcome, so I don't even try. Perfectionism causes clutter, throughout my environment and inside my head.

Ouch. I need a nap.

February 14: Valentine's Day. Ugh. This year I felt compelled to participate in two art swaps with Valentine themes. The exchanged artworks sit forlornly inside a decorated shoebox, waiting for me to dote over each one. I am unable to drum up the required enthusiasm.

I've got such a one-track mind lately; the tape loop of "Does it add value to my life? Is it related to my past, present or future?" is starting to grate on my nerves. Where, exactly, do these well-intentioned art swaps fit into my new, improved life? I want to honor the pieces I adore, and that can best be accomplished by letting go of the pieces that don't thrill me. When I have an empty bookshelf (does such a thing even exist, outside of home decor magazines?), I'll use it as a tiny gallery for the artworks I truly love. The rest, I close my eyes and toss. Sigh.

February 16: I find a cache of old paints in a drawer I haven't been able to access since my furniture arrived. They rattle when I shake them. Bye bye, cheap old paint! The tubes of good acrylics are harder to let go. I still cling to an imaginary future in which I actually know how to harness these incredible colors. I rationalize that a half-emptied drawer is better than a full-to-overflowing one.

How many darling travel-size watercolor sets does one girl need (especially a girl who doesn't use watercolors)? But I wish I were that watercolor-travel-journal girl. . . . I chuck the least attractive set in the "giveaway" box and return two to their drawer. Hey, it improves the situation by one-third. I choose to be proud of this small step.

February 17: Craptastic confession: I have a special drawer for empty beer cans which I'll someday transform into a fabulous crocheted beer can hat. Whaaaa?? For starters, I don't crochet. Beer can hats are lame. Will there be no beer cans in the future? Finally, why would I want to wear a sun hat made of heat-conducting materials? The beer cans go to the recycling bin. Sigh.

February 19: I tackle the overflowing bookcases. This is a tough one. I repeat this mantra: I am not my books. Owning the book does not mean that I own the knowledge inside it, and letting go of the book does not mean that I forever lose the opportunity for that knowledge.

I start with the cookbooks because it's so easy to find recipes online. There, one entire shelf is cleared! I carry them to my car so that I can donate them to the library tomorrow, before I have second thoughts.

Second thoughts come quickly. I retrieve the dog-eared copy of Martha Stewart's first publication. I ponder the wisdom of keeping Martha the perfectionist in my life. At least the pages are all stained.

February 20: Tonight I grow overheated as my mission gains momentum. Seeking relief, I step into the cool darkness of my yard to gaze at the moon, now half-disappeared into the earth's shadow: A total lunar eclipse is underway. I sense that this is a key moment in my month of intention. A little research reveals that eclipses are considered to be cosmic triggers, releasing pent-up energy and setting change in motion. Excellent, this is just what I need! This particular eclipse occurs on the cusp of Leo and Virgo, which one astrologer claims "emphasizes the discipline necessary to sustain creativity." Could it be any better? What a lucky sign! I race outside again to plant my feet firmly on the earth and turn my face toward the heavens, patiently waiting for the returning moonlight to illuminate my next steps.

February 21: I wake up with a perfect idea for the new art swap I've joined (I know, I can't help myself). The brief: Make artsy flowers in any media. The curveball: Make two sets of flowers, one to represent "before" and the other "after" (this is left open to interpretation).

Since perfectionism is on my mind, I decide that my "before" flowers will be lifelike ribbon roses in realistic colors, painstakingly crafted from French ribbon using traditional millinery techniques, because I used to believe that things had to look "real" and, if I was going to make something I should do it "right." By contrast, my "after" flowers will be playful and childlike and will eat into my stash of crazy print fabrics and fuzzy pipe cleaners. Bend, glue, trim, twist. Flower! No stress, no shoulders hunched in hushed concentration. No vision of a required perfect outcome.

To prove my point about the "after" flowers being fun and imperfect, I make them at the laundromat while twenty percent of my wardrobe goes through the wash cycle yet again. The constant questions from other patrons and the awkward working conditions add to their come-what-may charm.

February 25: To support and affirm my quest this month I decide to make prayer flags imbued with good wishes and composed of many layers of my precious fabrics.

You may have seen prayer flags flying from the eaves of Buddhist monasteries or strung along Himalayan mountain crests. Printed with holy texts, they are believed to release prayers into the universe as they deteriorate. The wind that whips them apart carries these spiritual energies to everyone it touches.

February 28: At lunch, someone tells me that clutter is nothing more than delayed decisions. As I exercise my neglected decluttering muscle, I find it easier to decide the fate of each bit of stuff. I tell myself: If it doesn't help me get closer to the life I want, it's not worth having. Now the challenge is that I am not sure what life I do want! I fear some of my dreams will die if I toss the things associated with them. But as the energy within and around me flows more freely, I grow confident that when creative ideas emerge, the necessary materials will be available. This month, I've come to trust that by subtracting unneeded stuff and old ideas, I add to my life immeasurably, and by ditching the troubling future and the imperfect past, I enhance my now.

Sheri's blog entry

March is roaring! We have not seen a winter like this in years. Snow, grey days and shoveling have left everyone ready for signs of spring. For me, I am pushing into my first of two deadlines for North Light. I will be heading out for the photo shoot on April 6 and the organization of getting ready has left me a bit frazzled. I can feel myself procrastinating, and I know this is often a result of feelings of overwhelm. When this starts to happen, it is time for a check-in. What is needed to move this energy? As I created my March intention page in my Book of Dreams, it became clear to me that I am in need of restoration. Yes, I have to keep working and meet my deadline, but if I continue to push this hard, it will actually have the reverse effect and I will end up being unproductive. I began the page by reaching, without thinking, for the color Pthalo Green. I love Pthalo Green; it's absolutely yummy. Green is the color of healing, hope, balance, serenity, freshness, birth and growth. I kept working, not "thinking" too much about where I was heading. A calendar showed up, flowers, an apple tree and a queen. And then this phrase, "The dance of the soul's journey, the promise of a new spring."

Two things have revealed themselves to me within this image. The first is that organization is key to help calm the feelings of overwhelm, especially because over half of the projects I will demonstrate during the photo shoot are those submitted by the Dream Circle artists and not projects of my own. It also reminds me that as I move into these final

months, I continue to need to replenish my well. Creating a visual image has allowed me to see what was underneath the overwhelm and find a helpful solution.

This month's intention: Replenish the Well.

March Dreamers
Jane and Thomas Wynn

The Devil is in the Details

A successful collaboration is achieved when there is an open stream of communication between the artists.

Creating and working on a collaborative project is a piece of cake. Well, if you like playing your luck, rolling the dice, or knowing where lightning will strike. It takes a lot of planning, not just in the beginning but throughout the entire process. You also need a good sense of humor, flexibility and constant motivation.

A successful collaboration is achieved when there is an open stream of communication between the artists. As we know, artists can be a fickle bunch, so at times this process can be a real challenge. Personality conflicts can be your biggest obstacle, but the end results of working in such a creative way can be very rewarding (or so I had heard!). I've often thought about collaborating on a project with my husband, Thomas, but admittedly, I've been skeptical about the chances of success, given that we have different approaches to the creative process. Hence, we both decided to set our intention on a successful collaborative project!

To begin the process, we first picked a restaurant that we both liked. I think that may have been the true beginning of this whole undertaking. We sat down to a lovely lunch at an Italian place with paper and pens in hand and we each began making two lists. One side of the paper had the words *Do Not Want* and the other side, *Want*. Strangely, it was easier for me to think of the things I did not want to do. I wrote that I did not want to make a shrine or just make something on paper or a painting on canvas. Thomas wrote that he did not want to journal or be committed to anything that involved handwritten words, or anything with wings or hats.

We both agreed that we wanted to try and stay away from things that seemed trendy, like using old photos. The positive things were actually a little more difficult to commit to. I started by writing the words *painting* and *sculpture* and he wrote *sculpt, build* and *kit-bash* (taking modeling kits, breaking them apart and using different pieces to create something brand new and completely independent of the original model). I loved this starting point. The hard part was forming these ideas into an actual project. As the meal was ending and I was ordering coffee, we finally came to the conclusion that we would create a narrative sculpture using skills that we were both good at and truly enjoyed. This felt good in my gut because we were approaching our intention from a place of joy and not dread; we would enjoy the process! The only catch was the pesky subject matter! What was this thing going to be about? Well, we have both

learned that when we get stuck, we turn to the Internet!

I came home and began searching for proverbs and common sayings for a starting point. I printed out a list of a variety of sayings and then picked out five of the ones I liked best. I gave the same list to Thomas and had him pick out his top five.

Over a lovely dinner of sushi a few days later, we sat and discussed our choices and decided on the best one for the project at hand. Our main criteria for judging these sayings were their ability to create an instant visual image. The one we chose was *An Idle Brain Is the Devil's Workshop*. I loved this the instant I saw it and Thomas had picked this out of his list as well. (I think that is what happens after many years of marriage—your brains become fused to one another!) Subliminally, I think one reason this felt so in line with our intention was that it made me think of the phrase, "the devil is in the details," and it was the details that we were apprehensive about working out so smoothly, so it was all highly appropriate.

So while in bed later that night, Thomas grabbed some paper and began doing what he does best, plotting and scheming! He started by drawing out his ideas in quick rough sketches, keeping in mind what was easily available in our collection of odd junk. We happened to have a plastic head form that he decided would make a perfect subject and base. This would be the anchor for the rest of the piece. Next was coming up with the devil and a workshop.

When the weekend came, we went out in search of dollhouse furniture because we knew it would make a perfect workshop. We found a table, a chair and some tiny tools. The devil would require a lot of conjuring in order to make this project work. While sorting though some containers of random stuff in my studio, I stumbled upon several plastic devil-head and also some Abe Lincoln-head swizzle sticks, which I had gotten from God knows where. It was totally meant to be! From this point on, it was only a matter of finding a body for this perfect head. We searched high and low, looking for a body to match. Hobby shops had some really nice army men that looked nifty so we bought a few boxes, and then we went to a cake decorating shop and found a groom that was even better, and so we bought him.

We took these plastic people home and placed them on the table to see which would make the best version of Satan and decided that the groom was the chosen one. (This was not a subliminal association, I assure you!) So Thomas took out a very sharp knife and performed a tiny human-toy sacrifice! He then connected the head to the body with a two-part, quick-setting epoxy. The two parts came together nicely and when he was finished, there stood the devil in all of his dark glory.

By this time, I stopped to realize that the collaboration thus far had been completely painless. Where were the disagreements? Was it actually this easy to work together on a single project, and we had just never before realized it? I didn't want to jinx anything, so I just kept continuing down my happy, collaborative road.

After the basic form was made, Thomas took the head form and using a Demel Tool, performed a simple lobotomy. The top of this head came right off, exposing a hollow form. He filled it in with expanding foam to make it sturdy. Once that had hardened and dried, he leveled the top flat with some sandpaper. He then traced the top of the head onto the piece of plastic card and cut it out with scissors. He glued it in place and went back and filled in any gaps. He finally sprayed it with a sandable primer spray paint.

I took over from here and went to work on painting details on the devil, the furniture, tools and even the big head form. I first gave a quick, allover coat of black sandable primer to the objects and then used "One Shot" enamel paint. I love this paint for the thickness and the coverage. Although it is a little difficult to work with at first, it can be blended and thinned nicely with some paint thinner. It covers all sorts of imperfections and creates a very pretty candy coating to any surface. I decided to tone down the glare of the shine with some liquid floor wax. I just dunked it, shook off the excess, and let it sit to dry. I did this with the furniture as well as those tiny tools.

When it came time to paint the large head form, I decided to give the surface an antique finish of rich gold and patina greens. I wanted it to look more like a mechanical head rather than a realistic human head. (I wanted to tell a story, not gross people out.) Metal paint worked great for this form. I applied several layers, allowing each one to dry before adding the next. I then added the patina liquid to the dried surface and watched the magic happen.

Finally, Thomas came back and set up the scene of the workshop. He managed to attach tiny seamstress pins to the bottoms of the pieces, added a tiny amount of epoxy for extra strength and when the position was determined, he pushed them into place. He cleaned the surface of any glue and handed it over to me for the details. I painted in shadows and highlights all over to make this piece come alive. I used regular lighting to help guide me as I painted. I looked for the natural shadows and exaggerated the highlights. This technique is similar to stage lighting and theater set designs. The two of us took a step back and made our last little adjustments and then called it a day.

It was complete.

We finished by going out for coffee and some delicious scones as a treat. While we ate, we talked about the entire process. We agreed that the reason everything seemed to go so well was that we were both secure with what the other person's strengths were and left one another to do the parts we could do best. By keeping our sights on the joy of the process and a successful outcome, we were able to sidestep territorial issues and such. Before we were finished, we came to the conclusion that we loved this process and decided to set our sights on a new project and a new intention. We understand that it might not always go this smoothly, but we both learned that by facing the fear of the unknown (a.k.a., not wanting to rock the boat that you share exclusive rights to) and attempting to work in a new way, remarkable things are possible—things that we wouldn't achieve as soloists. Although for the next go-around, we will take the high road, leave the devil to keep busy and give old honest Abe Lincoln a shot. . .

Sheri's blog entry

April snow showers . . . will they bring May flowers? That appears to be the question on everyone's mind right now after such a beautiful but long winter. On a walk this morning, I saw my first crocus poking its head up from a patch of mud and snow. What a surprise! As I get ready to leave for North Light next week, the symbolism did not escape me.

How blessed I felt to see that flower amidst the still, cold air. An offering of abundance and a reminder of the eleven-month cycle of seasons I have lived while writing this book. Instant joy, instant gratitude, instant abundance.

Abundance: What is the true meaning? Is it wanting more, acquiring more, asking for more? Or is it about something completely differ-ent, being grateful for even the smallest of things—like seeing your first crocus or hearing the first robin's song of the season? If I notice even the smallest of things each day, it will be an ever-present reminder to count my bless-ings. Noticing how abundant and full my life is right in this moment, without wanting or needing any more, also gives me a well to draw from if times are difficult.

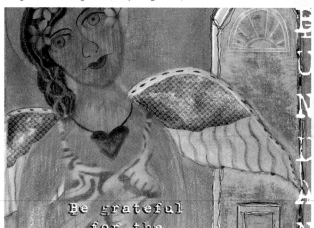

This month's intention: Abundance.

April Dreamer
Lesley Riley
Finding Meaning in the Bottom of a Bowl

I could fill many cups to overflowing with ideas, with art. What I want to do is to explore new styles, using bowls as the vehicle. But it's also a metaphor that ties it in with my other love, words.

Bowls—empty, small, delicate and white for babies. Large, powerful and bold—yet empty for the dying. Beautiful, colorful brimming bowls as we grow, embellished as we near our peak. Full to the brim with a graceful patina and a beautiful decay as we age.

Where do I focus my attention? What artwork will:
a) give pleasure?
b) create meaning?
c) allow discoveries?
d) teach me?

These are the questions I asked myself as I began my EnVision DreamTime. It didn't take me long to zero in on the fact that I wanted to explore one concept: empty vessels. Many years ago in a class with quilter David Walker, I began a quilt of seven bowls after a tarot reading he did for me. I had pulled the Seven of Cups card—a need to reflect upon choices. This card is a reminder to listen to out inner dreams and desires. How ironic then that this same message and symbol is reap-

pearing now during the EnVision process.

The quilt is unfinished. I don't need to finish it. At the time I was looking for my own voice. It was a bridge quilt, one I began in a style not my own, yet with the beginnings of what would eventually become my own. The bowl imagery had done its work. Now it was time again to see what the bowls held for me. I know so much more now about myself, my art, the unlimited well of creativity inside of me.

During my initial EnVision process I wrote, "I could fill many cups to overflowing with ideas, with art. What I want to do is to explore new styles, using bowls as the vehicle. But it is also a metaphor that ties it in with my other love, words.

"This exploration, using one concept, the bowl, will allow me to deviate into styles, color, abstraction, realism and so on. It's like a controlled experiment where one variable is constant. Then you do different things to it to see how it reacts.

"This makes the journey and the exploration of my desire to walk into other styles, as well as discover new ideas and new ways of working, much easier. Also—note to self—remember the desire to make my mark either through stitch or paint or . . . whatever."

So I set my intention: My intention for the month of April is to explore bowls in as many media, styles and dimensions as I can and see where it takes me.

During that initial EnVisioning process, time went by so fast. Just taking the first step made it all clear as to what to do. I was excited that I came up with a plan that gave me freedom, yet had parameters.

Is a basket a bowl?
Define bowl.
Fill my bowl with ideas; watch it overflow.
Figure holding bowl?
Large bowl in foreground and figure in background?

I began by devising a most simple pattern for a very basic bowl to be constructed from fabric. I know fabric, it's not the first thing people think of when they think of a bowl, but it was my plan to turn my favorite medium into a bowl. Fabric, paint and image transfer. I had envisioned it all in my head.

A lot of the time I don't move on an idea because I am—get ready—afraid of failure! There's a part of me that thinks I've got this one shot at getting something right and if I don't succeed then, I must abandon the idea. Yes, that's crazy. It's something I must overcome every time I try something new. With the EnVision Process, I had a sense of calm and courage because I knew this "bowl adventure" was all an exploratory process. The point was to try, to experiment, to go in different directions, and then to try some more, but always with the same focus—the bowl.

When you have a regular practice of focusing on a plan, a desire, it gives you a certain sense of comfort. It reigns in the scattered thoughts and activities. When your attention is focused on something specific, the universe complies by stepping up to meet you, sending signs, presenting opportunities and working alongside you. One of the things presented to me was this perfect quote:

Nothing can add more power to your life than concentrating all your energies on a limited set of targets.
—Nido Qubein

So I forged ahead with my fabric bowl. I was using three techniques that I was very familiar with, so I just had to do the work to bring it into reality. It turned out exactly as I had envisioned. I was elated. I was on a roll. I was eager to make more bowls, bigger bowls, to move on to refining my technique, imbuing the bowls with meaning and symbolism.

As the month wore on, the days rolled by and life butted in. I had originally requested the month of November for my EnVision month, but that time proved to be impossible. I figured by April my life would be smooth sailing. But does it ever turn out that way? Not for me so far. While my hands were full with babysitting my granddaughter, my mind was free to roam and plan. I created in my head until my hands were free. At night I would sketch. The symmetry of bowls takes practice—nuances of shading, perspective and point-of-view. The simplest object is often the hardest to capture in two dimensions.

I found another pattern option to try that would create a more rounded bowl, and I got it measured and cut. I began a journal: a touchstone and vessel for images of bowls, or objects that reminded me of bowls or sparked ideas for bowls. Creating in the journal became my daily activity while I waited for time to get messy in the studio.

In snippets of time, I cut bowl shapes from art board and prepped and painted them as studies for three-dimensional work. I mined old magazines for images and ideas, colors, textures and patinas. Questions arose: Why limit myself to fabric bowls? When is fabric not fabric? What could mimic fabric, or what could I create that would mimic fabric? Having just one thing to focus on helped reign in the overflowing array of "what-ifs."

Another DreamTime session led me to question this attraction I have to bowls. Here is my journal entry:

their shape, like a woman, curved
they symbolize the idea of anticipation,
possibilities, being filled—FULFILLED
their inside-outness
the smoothness
no beginning, no end

I answered Sheri's call to participate in *Creative Awakenings* because I knew that I would be searching for more meaning, new techniques and new directions in my art. The problem with starting anything new is that it is hard to know where to focus your energies and attention. I could have gone in so many directions. Like everyone, I am easily swayed by bright and shiny ideas, new techniques and supplies. But you don't get very far by flitting from one flower of an idea to the next. I was actually seeking a way to get in, to get to the heart of the yearning, and I believe my seeking is what prompted the universe to connect me with Sheri and this project.

Another bit of wisdom came my way during this process. I was chatting with Claudine Hellmuth about how and where to direct my energies and what to work on in my limited time. I have a long laundry list of things to do in this year off. Claudine said five words that have become my mantra: *Everything comes from the work.* And knowing what the work was, well that just sent me right into the studio with intention and purpose.

Throughout my month of intention—and even now—I felt empowered knowing that the intention I set at the beginning of the journey was such a guiding light along the way. By setting the intention to focus on only one thing, by limiting myself to the one thing, by having an assignment, so to speak, I was freed from having to walk into the studio and face a blank slate, an empty worktable. My mind didn't wander, no need to worry or wonder about what to do. I had my assignment and a plan of action. Create bowls. Any medium, mixing mediums, playing with size, texture, technique. Draw, paint, mold, sew, build, form, craft, MAKE. I gave myself permission to play. The intention was to see where creating bowls would take me. The bowls are the signs and symbols of my journey. I don't know where the journey ends (Is there an end? Should there even be an end?), but I know that each bowl is a step and each step propels the next. Moving forward is always good.

⑨ Transferring an Image onto Fabric

"Finding meaning in the bottom of a bowl." Doesn't that sound lovely? Lesley Riley shared with me her technique for making an ink-jet transfer onto fabric. This will support you in creating your very own intention bowl.

What You Need

- copy of bowl pattern, page 96
- scissors
- muslin or duck cloth
- pencil
- gel medium
- ink-jet transparency (not quick-dry)
- foam brush
- spoon
- acrylic paint
- pastel paints
- needle and thread
- textile hardener (Paverpol)

1 Cut out the bowl pattern with scissors. Trace the pattern onto muslin or duck cloth with a pencil.

2 After removing the pattern, sketch in the remaining part of the circle. Brush gel medium onto the portion of the fabric that will receive the transfer. Apply the medium as evenly as possible.

3 Set the transparency over the medium and burnish the portion of the image you wish to transfer with the back of a spoon. Use circular motions.

4 Peel up the transparency to reveal the transfer.

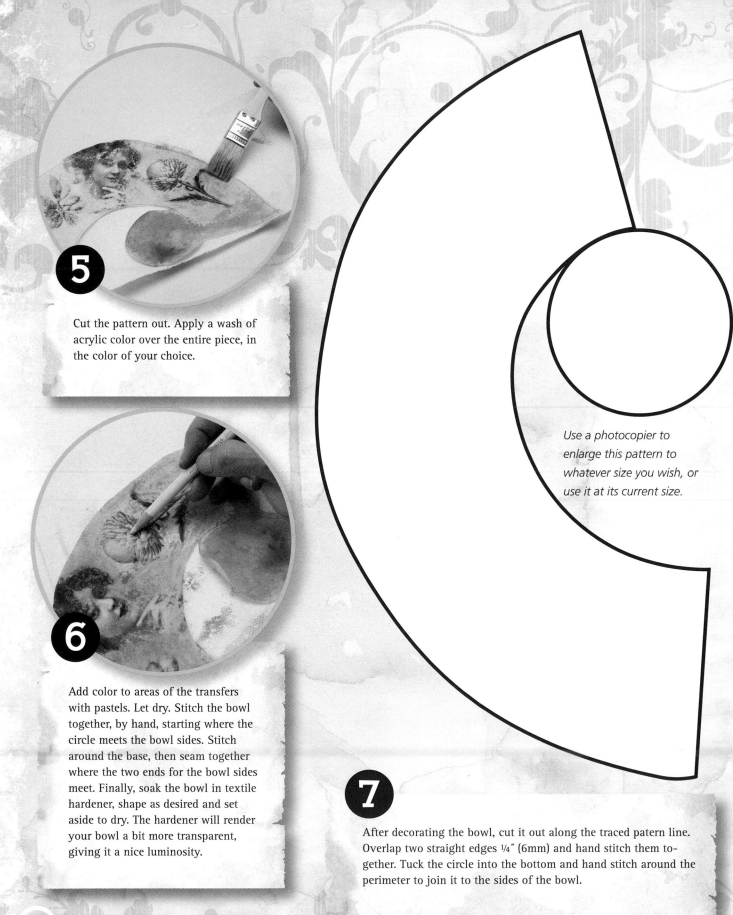

5

Cut the pattern out. Apply a wash of acrylic color over the entire piece, in the color of your choice.

Use a photocopier to enlarge this pattern to whatever size you wish, or use it at its current size.

6

Add color to areas of the transfers with pastels. Let dry. Stitch the bowl together, by hand, starting where the circle meets the bowl sides. Stitch around the base, then seam together where the two ends for the bowl sides meet. Finally, soak the bowl in textile hardener, shape as desired and set aside to dry. The hardener will render your bowl a bit more transparent, giving it a nice luminosity.

7

After decorating the bowl, cut it out along the traced patern line. Overlap two straight edges ¼″ (6mm) and hand stitch them together. Tuck the circle into the bottom and hand stitch around the perimeter to join it to the sides of the bowl.

Sheri's blog entry

It is May 1. Returning from North Light closed one door and left the final manuscript as the next door to walk through. As a result, April was a month of WORDS—reading words, cutting words, finding new words. I have lost all perspective and have no real idea how any of this will sound or be received.

I'm so grateful that I created a book circle in January. I knew I was ready for an audience; it was time to get the book out of my head and get some feedback, terrifying as that prospect was. Since January, my friends Beth, Cindy and Laura have given graciously of their time and brilliance. We meet every other week (Cindy by telephone) and hash things out with honesty. I am in awe of their linear minds; it has been so helpful for this somewhat-random woman. I owe these women a debt I hope I can one day repay.

I am grateful for the early months of writing solo. That I gave myself time to just write—without judgment, disregarding whether it made sense. I let myself SPILL, SPILL, SPILL. I jokingly told Tonia I thought I had written my opus; it was clear I had been holding things inside for a very long time. So spill I did, and now we find ourselves sifting and sorting to find the gems.

It has been easier than I would have imagined. Since I lost my perspective and feel too close to the book, I have no problem letting go of the words. They (my book group) are actually fearful we may cut too much, but now that I have spilled, I can see what is important—not all of it would be to a reader, only to me.

Aside from graduate school, this has been one of the biggest undertakings of my life. It might very well be my proudest accomplishment. It feels important as I complete this last month to look back on the year and of coming full circle to this moment.

This month's intention: Metamorphosis.

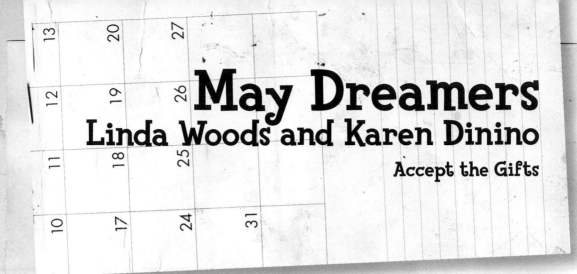

May Dreamers
Linda Woods and Karen Dinino
Accept the Gifts

You never know where your next gift is coming from—or from whom. One thing is certain, though: If you do not pay attention or take action, you can miss the gift altogether!

Being professional artists, writing books and sharing our joy in creative, free expression: These are our dreams come true. Even to us, it often seems these dreams became reality in a whirlwind. But in fact, dreaming didn't make them so. We chose to change our minds about how we experienced life, and our lives changed. We chose to take steps on our dream paths instead of gazing longingly at them. And we were amazed how short a time it takes for truly wonderful things to happen!

Our love of art journaling began when we were children, and blossomed when we were traveling as teens and adults. As kids, we used art as a shield against divorcing parents, shouting, shame and fear. We created journals to keep our real selves safe, journals that held powerful promises about who we were and would become, no matter what. Our art and words grounded us, providing stability among many earthquakes.

When we traveled later, our art journals evolved. Traveling, we slowed our pace, quieted our minds and felt safe to come out of hiding. We were constantly delighted by little things, looking for surprises around every corner. Unhindered by work, family or others' expectations, we could relax in the moment, literally stop and smell the chocolate—stop and sketch the chocolate!—and notice and partake of the kindness of strangers. We saw and heard gifts all around us, and we greedily accepted those gifts. After all, we were on vacation! Instead of being annoyed by traffic (as we would when at home), we took pictures of the crowded streets. Rather than cursing a missed train, we enjoyed coffee while doodling the pattern of the wrought-iron gates by the coffeehouse. We noticed that when on vacation, our creativity tripled, as did our energy. We filled art journals with inventive ideas, odes to the beauty of common days and mementos of laughter and love.

Hungry for this creative spark, we decided long ago that we could not wait for sporadic vacations; we chose to experience everyday life as if we were on vacation. We visualized ourselves as life explorers, traveling amongst our days for fun and learning. We envisioned being our dreams—being people who encourage others to create without fear, without rules, without limits. And then we did more than dream our future: We began by knowing we had already achieved it. This philosophy has made a huge difference in our creative energy and our happiness.

a cool breeze

shared laughter

sweet revelations

things wrapped with bows

moments of silence

ACCEPT THE GIFTS

This month, we realized that there is one aspect of "vacationing" that we want to express more: noticing and accepting gifts. In "real life," we tend to rush by gifts, or to deflect gifts, even those we give ourselves. We decided for a month to focus our intention on accepting the many gifts coming to us every day, if we just notice and accept them.

Linda started by designing beautiful journaled art to grab our intention, and call us to action. We talked about this perfect artwork first, so she could create something that would be meaningful to both of us. We both believe tulips are one of spring's best gifts, and she used colors with meaning for both of us. Orange and yellow are our comfort colors; purple is empowering; the blues fill us with hope. Together, we listed simple gifts we treasure and do not want to overlook. These gifts trigger memories in both of us, bringing up deep emotions that strengthen our intention to accept gifts. Linda titled the art with our specific plan for the month: *Accept the Gifts*. This plan presumes the gifts are here. There is no doubt about it, we just need to accept them. We each placed this art in our workspace (well, lucky Linda got to place the original art in her studio, and Karen received a lovely print. Apparently, Karen had not yet activated that "accepting the gifts" thing too well. . .) and we focused on it many times a day during the month.

Noticing the Gifts

You never know where your next gift is coming from—or from whom. One thing is certain, though: If you do not pay attention or take action, you can miss the gift altogether! By focusing on the *Accept the Gifts* art this month, we were tuned in to the gift channel, so to speak. We were definitely paying more attention to the many forms a gift can take, and we were even bolder in seeking gifts. One wonderful gift Karen received was compassion: Someone who could have made her life miserable instead "let her off the hook." Empowered by this month's intention, and by envisioning a gift, Karen stopped fearing and confidently expected compassion. Upon receiving it, she immediately fell off her chair in shock, but the key is, she noticed the opportunity for a gift, and then was open to receive it. In fact, she sought, and accepted, compassion *twice!* Compassion beats blame anytime.

Linda had similar experiences. Attuned to opportunities for gifts in many forms, Linda found that appointments opened in formerly all-booked schedules (when she asked), and that people happily said "Yes!" when she kindly and confidently invited them to help her. So often, we just do things ourselves, assuming that others do not have the time or inclination to give the gift of their help. In truth, people usually are happy and eager to help us, and we all have a lot of fun doing the work together! This gift of camaraderie and cooperation lightened many moments this month.

Accepting the Gifts

Typically, we are surprised by "gifts," and shower gratitude on those who give them. We enjoy sharing joy and giving to others, and being grateful feels good.

Having an attitude of gratitude starts a chain reaction—you start to see more to be grateful for. You start wanting to give more, to show your gratitude. This month, we realized the power of a sister proposition: An attitude of acceptance also starts a chain reaction. Suddenly, we had many opportunities to accept gifts.

We learned that *noticing* is not enough when it comes to gifts. Particularly as women, so many of us have been taught that it is not proper to actually accept the gift. Instead, we should be too busy to bother with such frivolity, deny that we are worthy, or immediately give the gift to someone else who needs it more. Often, we are just too tired to use a gift we've received. This month, more than ever, we proclaimed: Why dream big, wish with passion and plant fertile seeds if we are too busy, tired or humble to accept the gifts? We vowed to accept every gift offered to us, period. Even if it made us uncomfortable, even if we knew someone else who could use it, even if we should be working, even if, even if, even if. We were shocked, yet challenged, by the actual gifts that arrived. It sounds silly, but it is true. From flowers to concert tickets to job opportunities to great parking spots, we received many wonderful chances to accept gifts. We fought the habit to say, "Oh, no thank you, I can't accept that!" We accepted.

And a fantastic thing happened: The more we accepted, the more we had to give. At times, we were overflowing with energy and creative excitement—just like when we travel to a new place. We expanded our networks of friends, discovered new territory, and gained ideas and perspectives we cannot wait to share. We had avoided and rejected gifts in the past, with silly thoughts that we should not accept them or would diminish ourselves by "taking" from others. The opposite is true.

We and others were enriched by this experience, because everyone actually received a gift in the process.

Creating *Accept the Gifts* art reminded us to DO something different this month, to open our minds and our eyes in a new way, to ask for what we need, and to say "YES!" to gifts. Probably the greatest gift we received is the gift of balance. We experienced that giving and receiving are equally valuable and necessary arcs of the same circle. When the world sends us tulips, we will humbly accept the gift!

Sheri's blog entry

Awakenings. It is finally spring here in Colorado, still snowing and cold some days, but the truth of the season lives in the flowers and trees that courageously stand tall in search of light and warmth. I relate, as I feel like Persephone rising from the underground, wiser, stronger and no longer naïve. In being a daily witness to my own life over these last twelve months, I have learned more about myself than almost any year prior. I can look back and see that I have experienced almost unimaginable personal transformations. Writing this book has been my greatest life teacher. In doing so, I have truly learned to trust the process.

June brought with her several surprises. Upon completion of the book, we unexpectedly found our new dog, a beautiful black Lab named Sir Blue Moon Fescue. It has been four years since our last Lab passed on, and we have not considered another dog until finding Blue.

Sir Blue brought with him an unexpected blessing, an opportunity to share the news of his arrival with my husband's Aunt Annie, who had been battling cancer for the last several years. She was so happy for us, and she laughed with us as we shared the story of finding him. Later that evening, Annie began to slip in and out of this world, as she began to cross the bridge to her next journey. We have been told that our story of Blue is one of the last clear conversations she had. We feel so grateful to have shared the news of this event with her, knowing the joy it brought to her, as dogs were a bond she and Andy shared.

I am grateful Annie knew about this book. I know she was very proud of me. I am grateful she was able to see the mixed-media piece I created for Gypsy Spirit Days with her mother's image in front of her beloved old Woody. I only regret I will not be able to sit on the back porch in Russell and read the pages aloud to her in front of the apple tree we planted during our vow ceremony.

As always, I am reminded that life is fragile. Take nothing for granted. Always let those around you know they are loved, cherished and adored. Tell them how they have added to your life; thank them for the gifts they have given you. Leave nothing unsaid and you will always find peace.

Birth, death, the cycle of life—when you live your life in the present moment, in full awareness of the twelve-month cycle, you realize how many of these events you experience in a lifetime. The circle of life is a constant and we grieve only if we have loved intensely. What other choice is there?

Laura's essay about creating intention in the landscape is the perfect story to end this journey of a thousand miles, as it is now time to move into the landscape of my life.

June Dreamer
Laura Kirk
Awakenings

Creative Awakenings
a process of
creative discovery,
exploration,
patience and acceptance
surrounded
in a circle of
friendship
where self-doubt
gives way
to truths and dreams
that lie within
and
prepares the soul
for journeys
yet to
come.

Opening the Gate

When Sheri first asked if I would contribute to her book, I said yes, but I didn't really take her seriously. I figured that she was just being nice; now I'm not sure what I was thinking because I know Sheri much better than that. And when she asked again, I realized that this was for real and it was time to show up and walk the talk.

As I have thought about my contribution to this book, I have been reminded and guided by something that Sheri once said. She said that at some point in our creative journey, there comes a time when we know all the techniques—well, a lot of them, anyway—and we need to move in a new direction. We need to begin to find our own voice so we can find our own way. We need to look inside and trust what is within. It is at this point that we have to leap—believing in ourselves, in the work that we have done to that point and in the support that we have from others.

It is at this place that I find myself now. Ready for a leap, ready to share a seed that has been growing in me for many years. Afraid and yet energized and buzzing with anticipation.

I am a landscape architect, gardener, writer, artist, mother, wife, friend and colleague. As a former student of Sheri's class, I have witnessed firsthand the power of the creative process to transform my own life as well as those of others.

Prior to the class, I was unsure of my creative abilities, but I'm different now. When I engage in the creative process, I respond to the daily challenges of life with more patience and compassion. I feel my inner strength and power. I see possibilities instead of obstacles. I connect with my intuitive voice and allow that to be my guide.

It took me quite a while to form a rhythm for my creative play. Sheri recommended squeaking in thirty minutes every day, but that never worked for me. What did work was dedicating each Friday to my creative journeys, and it has made all the difference.

Right now, I'm sitting in my studio—a room of my own, a place I can dream and continue to explore the creative process. In this room, I'm surrounded by the sense

that anything is possible. As I work and play, I dance with delight, unable to move fast enough, and there's no plan—no preconceived outcome.

Sheri suggested that I explore the idea of creating intention in the landscape. This resonated with my roots as a landscape architect and my passion for it as it exists in all of its forms. For as long as I can remember, my sense of being, my spirit and my dreams have been defined by my connection to the land. The landscape has a certain sacred quality about it, offering the potential for renewal, reflection and inspiration. I see myself as a facilitator, bringing the landscape alive to others, helping them find and feel a connection with the land. My greatest goal is to share this vision with others.

Contributing to this book has offered me a way to clarify my vision. Once I started, the writing flowed from somewhere unknown. I guess it must have been there waiting to be released. I didn't have an outline or an idea of what I was going to say or how I was going to say it. It just came.

The visual manifestation of this process has taken shape in many forms. My room is alive with collages, paintings, quotes and canvases of all shapes and sizes. Images of the landscape are embedded throughout. If I could, I would share the entire room with you as it captures the power of my transformation. But with the assistance of my family, I have chosen one piece. It's an intention garden of sorts. The trees beckon through the swaying of their branches. Once I allowed myself to open the gate, I could hear them and respond to their call with offerings that glisten in the light. As I entered into these woods, what I discovered was that my body was warmed by the sun, my mind was stilled, and my soul was readied to explore the garden of my dreams with intention, purpose and joy.

This is the seed that I would like to share with you.

Creating Intention in the Landscape

As I have traveled on this journey, I have found that sometimes a journal page just isn't big enough to capture my creative explorations. Sometimes a wall isn't big enough. It is the landscape that calls to me.

And so, my question to you is, what about moving out into the landscape as both a place for inspiration and a place for expression? We can engage with the land in ways that are big and bold or small and subtle, for our own reflection or to be shared with others. I have found that there are an infinite number of ways to express intention in the landscape—some traditional, some not so; some are active, some are passive. Come with me while I explore a few.

Get Outside

Whether living in an urban or rural environment, there is always some sign of nature just outside the door. Open the door and take a look, or better yet take a walk. Find a bench in a neighborhood park or a smooth rock at the river's edge and just sit for a minute. Listen, smell, see, feel, breathe. Even in the city, there is something waiting to be noticed: the chirp of a bird, a green blade of grass, a flowering shrub, a squirrel racing up a tree. In that moment of rest and awareness, set an intention—a word, a thought, an action—and let that intention be a guide for the rest of the day, the week, the month, the next twelve months. Return to that place over time to revisit that feeling, that moment, and check in to see how things are going. Take a picture of something that moved you while sitting there and tape it to your refrigerator or bathroom mirror or closet door as a reminder of that moment of reflection. Bring home a pebble or a leaf that has fallen from a nearby tree and put it by your bedside so that it's the first thing you see each morning and the last thing you see at night so that your daydreams and night dreams are filled with that intention.

Let It Grow

Plant an intention, nurture it and witness its growth. Begin with a seed, or a seedling, or a small tree, and watch it change and evolve and flourish with time and care. Choose the seed with care: Pick a favorite color, or a strikingly fragrant smell, or something that radiates in the fall, or a deliciously flavored fruit or vegetable. Select a plant that corresponds to the depth of the intention: Should it bloom in a month, or once a year or over a lifetime? Is it wild or tame? From such a simple beginning, just a seed not even as big as the tip of the pinkie finger, watch something beautiful and rich and full of pleasure materialize. It can happen anywhere: in the yard, in a window box outside the kitchen window, in a pot by the front door. But put it somewhere important within the patterns of your everyday life and take notice as it grows and changes.

I was walking today along my favorite route out of our small mountain town and up the neighboring hill. The landscape on the hilltop always takes my breath away; it's so open, free and spacious. The adjacent fields were covered in a fresh layer of snow, and they called to me just like a clean sheet of paper in my journal. I hopped the fence and wrote LEAP in the fields with my footprints. It was so fun and grand and filled me with courage to move forward into my dreams. Now, I don't know if my writing will still be there in an hour, or a day, but I know the memory of that moment will travel with me for well beyond today. I have a picture of it in my heart and soul and that picture will last.

There are so many ways that we can write our intentions in the landscape: with our footprints in the sand, with a stick in the mud, with a pile of leaves or flower petals on the lawn. Collect a handful of pinecones or sticks. It can happen anywhere, anytime. If there's a camera handy, take a picture. If not, just that act of interacting with the body and the land will travel with you. And if the wind blows it away in an hour or it snows another three inches and covers it up, the spirit of that intention will still live on.

Create a Ritual

How about a ceremony in the landscape? The ceremony could take on many themes: healing, forgiveness, letting go, birth, celebration, connection. It could be a ceremony for one, or two, or many. It could be a response to the passing of the seasons, or the time of day, or an event—planned or spontaneous. It could be a permanent mark in the landscape or something that changes and passes with time. It could be an opportunity to set a personal intention, or to share an intention with a trusted group of friends to cement a collective intention. Here are a few ideas.

What about a tree wrapping ceremony? Grab some crepe paper streamers from the grocery store in varying colors, gather a group of friends at a playground or a park or a friend's home, and start wrapping the tree trunks. And watch what happens. Suddenly the trees are alive—art pieces in the landscape. Or were they always that way and we had just stopped noticing? This could be a great activity for a Creative Awakenings Circle (see page 82).

How about a ceremony to let go of fear or anger or hurt or whatever else it is that gets in our way? Buy a helium balloon at the grocery store, choose a favorite color and go to a quiet spot. Take some time to settle and reflect, decorate the balloon, write all over it, pouring out your thoughts. Then let it go and watch it sail. I've done this before, and I promise it works. When you release that balloon, something shifts inside and you are able to exhale the confusion that has stifled you.

The possibilities for ceremonies in the landscape are limitless. In my hometown, a group of women gathers every month on the night of the new moon. Each month they meet at a different house. The hostess for the evening chooses some way to celebrate the cycle of the moon as a manifestation of our connection to the earth and the universe around us. One night, every woman received a pebble upon arrival, and one by one they dropped their pebbles into a wading pool that had been filled with a couple of inches of water. As each woman dropped her pebble, her private intention was carried forth through the ripple of water and held sacredly in the collective energy of the circle of friendship and community. It didn't take much: pebbles, a moon, a wading pool, some water and a circle of women. But from those simple ingredients came something profound, lasting and transforming.

Incorporate Others

Sometimes in setting our intentions and moving into our own dreams, we create this cascading effect, providing an opportunity for others to move forward as well. Everyone has to find her path and her time on her own, but sometimes watching and observing others provides a sense of inspiration or a flicker of hope: If they can do it, maybe I can, too. Sometimes, in marking something that has moved us, we create an opportunity for others who pass by to stop and take notice as well. In the West, a common way to mark trails is by making a small cairn, or a collection of pebbles or rocks. What about making a small cairn in the landscape that might call someone's attention to a beautiful view or smell, flower or collection of leaves? We can never know for sure whether or not anyone else will stop at that place and experience that setting in the same way, but it might give someone a moment to pause, to step out of his daily routine, to notice something new and reflect on his surroundings in a different way.

It reminds me of a story that Sheri once recounted. She likes to take walks by the river near her house. One day as she was walking, she noticed that someone had had great fun collecting pebbles and arranging them sequentially on a fallen tree limb. How long they had been there or by whom they were placed, she will never know. But on that day she noticed them and experienced her walk, and that place on the trail, in a different way. Whatever she was thinking at that moment, her thoughts were interrupted and shifted as she found herself caught up in her discovery. The next day, Sheri returned with a friend and her child and they added to the pebbles. And so it goes.

Build It

What about creating an intention garden in your own yard, on your front porch or on your balcony? It could be big or small depending on your space and inclination. Maybe it's a place for restful contemplation, or spirited adventures. There might be a spot to sit in the warmth of the winter sun. The view could be inward or borrowed from the distant landscape. The space might feel protective or expansive. You might walk by it every day on the way in and out of your home, or perhaps it's a little out of the way. Maybe it's a place to sit with your journal and write, draw, paint or collage. Does it have a table? Or perhaps there's a small sandbox that you can leave a message in, or decorate with smooth colored pieces of glass—take a picture, use it in your journal and then when you're ready, begin again. There could be a chalkboard hanging on the fence, or a shiny piece of metal with magnetic letters and words, or a tree hung with ornaments that chart your journey. Is it just for you or can others see it? Your intention garden could be surrounded by plants that require tending so that the act of gardening is a part of the experience. Do the plants provide a backdrop as a place for rest and meditation, or do they arouse the senses with beautifully bright colors and fragrant smells? Start small and then watch the change as the patterns of time and season give way to the unfolding of your dreams.

Begin Anew

It's hard to begin. The Toad Committee that Sheri speaks of can be vocal. I know that for me, the Toads come in all shades of fear and can stop me cold before I ever get going. And in a funny way, beginnings have no end; once we begin, there's some other beginning waiting around the corner—another canvas, another sheet in the journal, another dream. But beginnings make us feel alive, even if we're afraid. So I end where I started: Get outside and set an intention in the landscape. It may feel awkward or uncomfortable at first, but in connecting with nature we find an opportunity to connect with the inner calling of our being and sow the seeds of our *Creative Awakenings*. Come with me as I step outside; I'm off to live my dream. I'm going to begin by playing in the dirt and building a labyrinth in the landscape with a group of women I love and adore.

The Transformation Deck and Your Next Twelve Months

We all know that creating a dream is a HUGE leap of faith. Holding on to your dream without letting it wilt or fall by the wayside can sometimes be a bit challenging. Hence, I have created the Transformation Deck to help you circumnavigate any Toad, dancing gremlin and/or personal challenge that might show up on the road to your dreams. The deck has been created to help you stay on track and inspired even if there are—and trust me, there will be—one or two potholes in the middle of the road.

As you begin to shed the layers that have kept you from reaching for your dreams, you will likely notice old patterns and habits surfacing and in dire need of attention. For me, writing this book was like stepping into the movie *Jumanji* with Robin Williams. In the movie he finds a game, starts to play and the game becomes *real.* On the road to this long-held dream of mine, I honestly encountered almost every one of my life challenges, including but not limited to: fear, self-doubt, shame, procrastination and creative block. It was as if the Universe was delivering the exact experiences I would need to overcome my nagging issues, move to another level of personal growth and help me remember what others will experience in the realm of reaching for a dream.

The Transformation Deck offers you creative exercises, journal writing, storytelling, adventure and personal-challenge techniques to support your process and motivate you to action! There are twenty-four cards in the deck. I created the art you see on the deck in response to intentions I set for myself while writing *Creative Awakenings*. Each month I used my Book of Dreams to create and set a personal intention, based on what I was feeling as I stepped into the month. As a result, there are cards that will call you to adventure, cards that will offer you personal and professional challenges and cards to help you transform a particular issue. All in all, the deck is intended to offer you an opportunity for a creative adventure of one kind or another. You may find the deck I have created sufficient for your journey, or you may be inspired to create your own based on your own personal experiences, so I have included instructions for making your own personal Transformation Deck on page 129.

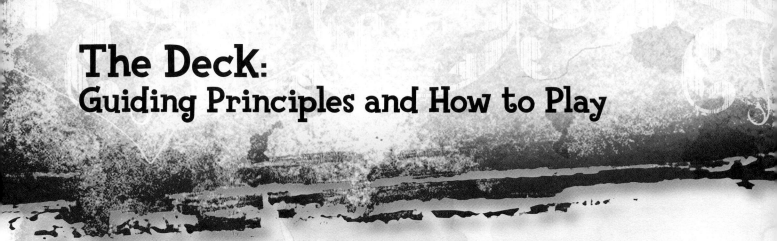

The Deck:
Guiding Principles and How to Play

The Transformation Deck has six guiding principles: EnVision It, Create It, Believe It, Write It, Live It and Re-EnVision It. The principles are creative jump-starts with activities designed to inspire action. There is no particular order to the principles, and not every principle is used on every card. Using your Book of Dreams to work with the principles gives you a place to answer the call!

The Creative Awakenings Guiding Principles

EnVision It: A relaxing interactive practice to discover and create intention with your mind. *EnVision It* will help you begin seeing the symbols of your unconscious.

Create It: The art of intention is a tangible, creative process. This step works hand in hand with the *EnVision It* principle. *Create It* activities will take your dreams from random scattered ideas to visible, tangible and concrete concepts.

Believe It: Set your purpose and attitude in the direction of your stated intention. Try it on! Imagining yourself taking those steps will support your psyche in knowing your dream is possible. If need be, act "as if" and "fake it 'til you make it!"

Write It: This principle is to support you in hearing your own voice. The journal practice is there to help you see the limitless possibilities, as well as any objections or perceived challenges that might be in the way. It is very important to get any objections out onto paper (or onto your computer), so they are not spinning around in your mind. Getting it out and getting it down gets you past it.

Re-EnVision It: Re-EnVision the challenges and fears that bind you. Simply put, this step will change your thought process. As you uncover old inherited or implanted stories and if your personal Venomous Toad Committee keeps inviting itself over for tea, you will create new stories and loving affirmations that inspire and energize you.

Live It: Now is the time for action! You have used the principles and practice to change your beliefs and thinking. Now it is time to become an active participant in the process.

How to Play

I suggest you use the Transformation Deck with your Book of Dreams, as I did. Remember, your Book of Dreams is your guidebook for adventure, so it is the perfect place to work through the challenges and emotions you will experience while reaching for your dreams. At some point, however, you may find you need to break out of the confines of your Book of Dreams. *Go for it!* Create larger mixed-media pieces if you are ready for a larger canvas, as I did with *Gypsy Spirit Days* and *Dare To Be Feisty!*

1. Shuffle the deck. As you are shuffling, allow your mind to relax and let go of any chatter. As you are shuffling the deck, allow a question to surface that you would like answered, or simply allow your subconscious to guide you.

2. Lay cards facedown on a surface or spread them out in your hands. Allow your intuition to guide you, and pull out one of the cards.

3. Each design on the card is embedded with a number. When you pull a card, turn it over and match the

The Card Index

number to the corresponding page in this book. Turn to that page and read how to reignite your dream!

Travel Advisory: Have you lost your way? Has the road become foggy or filled with potholes? A perfect way to use the deck is to find new direction.

In lieu of Steps 1 and 2 above, you can use the Card Index on this page as your guide. This index gives you an opportunity to use the cards to work through a specific issue or challenge. For example, let's say you wake up and you are feeling blocked, or you're procrastinating on a project that needs to get started. You can use the index to find the card (such as Unlock the Block) that can support you in a transformation around that particular challenge!

Field Note

Here are some other ideas for how to play.

• Use the deck for the full twelve-month process, pulling one card every month to help you set your intention.

• Use the deck as part of your Everyday Bliss Ritual (see page 118), pulling a card each day for encouragement to reach for your dreams.

• Use the card index to search for a particular card if you are feeling stuck, blocked or facing a particularly difficult personal challenge. Find the card that suits your needs in the deck and use the principle to help you move forward.

Believe

If you received this card today, you might be in the flow and astounded at the progress you have made so far. Congratulations for making a commitment to believe in your shining brilliance and wealth of talent. Belief in self is a major aspect to reaching for your dream!

If you pulled this card but are not yet seeing the fruits of your labor, don't despair—this card is for you, too. Remember, dreams need time to incubate. Don't give up now. Hang on, don't lose faith, put on your feistiest shoes, dance your fear, and keep walking toward your dreams!

Having a guide or mentor (actual or imagined) who has walked the path before us can offer us fresh ideas and clues to new possibilities. One of my inner guides is a woman with long, grey hair who sits on a cliff surrounded by her power animals.

EnVision It: EnVision an image of a mentor or guide who will help you believe.

Create It: Create an archetypal collage of your guide or mentor in your Book of Dreams.

Write It:
• Pull out your Milestones Passport and take fifteen minutes right now to celebrate your success, no matter how small. You are going to write yourself a pat-on-the-back letter. Begin with this statement: "Look at you grow! I am celebrating you today because you have. . ."

• Your guide has come to visit today and has some wisdom to share with you. Using your nondominant writing hand, begin writing with this statement: "I believe in you because. . . "

Live It: What steps would you have to take in order to make your dream a reality? Create a stepping-stones map. In your Book of Dreams draw a path with pebbles. On each pebble write the intention that will move you toward your stated intention.

Imagine the Possibilities

Pretend you are a famous journalist, and I have sent you to get the exclusive story of one of the most successful people in the country. What do you want to know? Details, details, juicy details!

Find someone tangible to interview, someone in your personal circle who has stepped successfully into his or her dream, or someone you may not know yet but have come to admire—maybe someone whose blog you enjoy reading, or someone else you've met through the Internet.

Write It: Create a list of dream questions you want to ask, such as:
1. How were you able to take the leap?
2. What were your emotions at the time of the leap?
3. What kind of research did you do ahead of time?
4. Did you write a business plan?
5. Did you take out a business or personal loan?
6. Looking back, what has been the greatest gift about taking the leap?
7. If you had any words of wisdom for a fellow dreamer, what would they be?

Live It: Pick a date for your interview and invite your subject for lunch or coffee, or make an appointment for a telephone or e-mail interview. Let them know what you are up to so they don't feel ambushed. If you are doing a local interview, have someone take a photograph of you and your subject to place in your Milestones Passport.

Create It: With your interview answers, create a Reach for the Stars Collage in your Book of Dreams. This will be a visual representation of what it would look like to take your own leap. Don't leave anything out. Imagine this has already transpired and everything is in place. Let go of fears about finances, change, consequences, etc. None of that matters here; you simply have to know what is true in the deepest place of your heart.

Shadow/Light

Embracing shadow aspects (the parts of self that remain largely hidden from our conscious mind) can be one of the most healing experiences of your life journey. Left hidden without an attempt on our part to understand them, shadow aspects can manifest as negative emotions and patterns that will often sabotage our dreams. Very often when these shadow aspects are revealed, we look upon them negatively and attempt to repress the feelings they bring, instead of accepting the feelings as part of a duality—the duality of light and shadow inherent in each of us.

When light shines on the shadow, a golden gem is revealed. Like the lotus that grows out of moist, dark mud, nothing can grow without a bit of darkness, along with a healthy dose of light.

Create It: Create a collage in your Book of Dreams dedicated to your shadow aspects. A visual representation of these aspects will help you acknowledge and understand them, offering you an opportunity to bring them into balance and find the golden gems.

Write It: How have these aspects defined you to date, and how might they be holding you back from your dreams and intentions?

Re-EnVision It: Now is the time to shine a light on your shadow aspects. Imagine standing in a garden, the sun shining on your face. Just behind you a shadow is cast. You turn and look back; a golden gem is waiting for you in the soil. What does it reveal to you? Create another collage and/or writing entry in your Book of Dreams.

Releasing the Reins

When first learning to ride, there is a tendency to pull hard on the reins because we haven't yet found our center point and don't know how to use our legs properly. This pulling instinct is actually an awkward attempt to find balance. The result is pretty darn confusing for the horse because the tendency is to be frantically kicking and pulling at the same time, implying that we want to go forward. The result? The harder we pull, the more the horse struggles and around in circles we go, until we find a way to *let go of the reins!* Where do we start? It is all about trust. When you finally develop a trusting relationship with the horse and with yourself, the ride is much smoother and much more fun.

Which leads us to the topic of negative control. Notice I said *negative* control. Is there a positive side to control? Sure, like everything else, control has both a shadow and golden side. An example of the golden side of control is discipline. Discipline is an element of control that allows us to carry out tasks and intentions successfully. Negative control is the shadow side. It's the illusion that if we pull hard enough on those reins, we will be able to control each and every aspect of life. Generally speaking, this is a big setup for disappointment—not to mention anxiety—and the art of letting go is about finding the center point in the saddle of your life.

Write It: Identify the areas in your life that reflect the shadow side of negative control.

Create It: Create a self-portrait (like the one portrayed on the deck) depicting an image of you riding a wild horse, balanced in the saddle and letting go of the reins.

Live It: What small steps can you take this week to begin to let go of the reins?

The Toad Committee

Like terrifying, flying monkeys racing through the darkening sky on their way to Oz, inside each of one us are gremlins and inner critics just waiting to voice their nasty opinions! These Toads will generally show up when you step out of your comfort zone and feel vulnerable. I generally have a symphony of croaking voices in my head and have named my inner critics "The Venomous Toad Committee." I am sure you have your own your committee, but it's time to tame the Toads and help them find touchstones to the truth!

The most important thing you can do is *hear them out.* Turn up the volume and listen to each and every one of their concerns. Once you have tuned into your own Toads, you might discover something very surprising: Their clamor might actually be concern for your safety and well-being and not intended to malign or scare you!

Once you have listened to their concerns, there is room for negotiation. Use the guiding principles below to support this very important transformational activity.

Create It: The collage on this card depicts my own Venomous Toad Committee. Create a depiction of your committee in your Book of Dreams.

Write It: Over the next week, make notes in your journal each time you are in touch with your Venomous Toad Committee. Writing with your *dominant* hand, begin by asking the Toads: "As I take this small risk to reach for my dream, what would help you feel more secure?" Respond by writing the answer with your *nondominant* hand. Keep writing until you feel you find clarity.

Live It: Share with your Toads your touchstones to truth. A touchstone to truth is what you know to be true in the deepest place of your heart, when you step away from fear and doubt. For example, "I am smart and intelligent and not prone to making impulsive or irresponsible decisions." Place your touchstones to truth on sticky notes around your house.

Random Acts of Inspiration

If you received this card today, the muse is tickling your heart and desires a creative flight of fancy. Your assignment is to pay it forward with a random act of creative inspiration, ingenuity and imaginative genius! This idea was inspired by my friend Amber Sparkles, an amazing poster artist who lives in my town. You can check out her work and Web site at www.ambersparkles.com.

Create It: Find an expired poster, postcard or advertisement on one of those overcrowded bulletin boards in supermarkets found across the country. Change it up and apply your random creative inspiration by adding your own doodles, photocopies, paints and ephemera.

Write It: Here are a few ideas for random acts of inspiration: Write an inspiring poem, mantra or slogan on your appropriated art piece and use it to brighten up someone's day. Or help a friend unlock a creative block by creating an inspirational assignment for them and send it via snail mail.

Live It: Leave a random act of inspiration (such as an artist trading card you create yourself) anonymously at someone's home, workplace or on their car windshield. Or send a piece of art via snail mail. If you're confronted about your random act, DENY, DENY, DENY. It's much more fun that way!

Create a New Story

WE ALL HAVE A STORY WAITING TO UNFOLD

Along with our Venomous Toad Committee, many of us retain what I call inherited or implanted stories—stories handed down to us over the many years of our lives. Many of these stories add positive value to our lives. Others are like big bad fairy tales, except they involve real-life experiences and people and places we know. If these stories and their resulting beliefs remain unquestioned, they will keep you from knowing your true potential. Creating a new story involves an inner excavation. Find the stories from your history that you value and want to keep, and lay to rest those that may not belong to you, no longer serve you and perhaps never have. It is not about finger pointing or blame. It's about claiming and writing a story that is your very own.

EnVision It: Use the EnVision Art of Intention Process on page 21 to uncover your inherited and implanted stories. Don't worry about the sources or finding blame. Your job is just to uncover them.

Write It: Make a quick list of stories that might be keeping you from your dreams even if you can't remember who told them to you.

Live It: Create a ritual that will support you in letting go of the old stories that no longer serve you and will celebrate the stories that add value to your life.

Re-Envision It: Create a new story! Be patient; you might have to dig deep. Writing in the third person can help you break through the inhibitions of writing about yourself in a positive way (i.e., "She was a woman who. . .").

Believe It: What is the rallying cry of your new life story? Write this in your Book of Dreams.

Replenish the Well

LOVE THY MUSE... REPLENISH THE WELL

We all know what it's like to try and force creativity—to sit before the blank computer screen, blank canvas or empty garden bed, staring ahead, hoping and praying—oftentimes sweating under a time crunch—that something will reveal itself. The truth is, your muse may be having a temper tantrum because she needs a break and you haven't been listening. A creative mind needs time for rest and rejuvenation, playfulness and even a nice dose of inactivity to refresh and regenerate. It is time for a muse vacation. Let's give her a break and replenish her well.

EnVision It: Stop everything and relax. Begin by closing your eyes and taking some deep breaths. Put your hand on your belly; make sure your breath is moving past your chest and reaching the pit of your stomach. Exhale through your mouth—don't be shy, make some noise! You will soon feel relaxed and able to tune in.

How do you know what your muse needs? Listen to her. She might be whispering because she thinks you will argue with her, so you might have to listen closely. I promise, she is there.

Write It: What did she tell you? What does she need today to replenish the well?

Live It: Here's what I do when the muse needs a vacation, to keep her from overspending.
- Free: Get your creative endorphins in gear. Get out in nature!
- Free + the price of a cup of coffee or tea: Go to a bookstore/cafe with an awesome alternative magazine section and fill your journal with juicy new ideas.
- Half a tank of gas or foot powered: Head out for a Gypsy Spirit Day (see page 117).

Hint: Keep a list of Muse Vacation ideas at the ready in your Book of Dreams.

Unlock the Block

In any inspired life, there will be moments when you experience uncertainty about direction or, worse, a full-on creative block. Creative blocks often happen at the worst times—such as when you're facing a deadline (like writing a book!). This can induce feelings of panic. When you are blocked, it is important to have tools to help. I have just the tools for you to excavate the buried treasure locked in your heart.

Live It: Begin with a Wild Heart Treasure Hunt. You can take a solo flight or invite your Dream Circle (see page 132). The full treasure hunt guide can be found at the Creative Awakenings Salon (www.creativeawakeningscommunity.com). Go out and gather objects you consider out of your comfort zone, things you would normally never hang in your home or studio—postcards, magazines, bumper stickers, found objects and so on. Push your boundaries. You can do your treasure hunt over the course of a day or a week.

Create It: With your gathered treasure at hand, it's time to create an EnVision Board of Inspiration! For this you will need a large bulletin board or a piece of foamcore. Now it's time for a Wild Heart Jam Session. Set a timer for fifteen minutes. Intermingle the out-of-your-comfort-zone items. Without thinking too much about it, tack your favorites to your board in groups. Set the timer again for three minutes. Looking at your board, write random words that come to mind.

Re-EnVision It: Reflect on your Wild Heart Jam Session for at least a week and review the list of words you created. Capture and journal the subtlest of ideas. It all counts, even—and especially—if they feel outrageous or avant-garde.

Abundance & Prosperity

Are the pieces in place for your dream to flow in the way of *abundance and prosperity*? This is not only about creating financial consciousness and a strong foundation to stand upon, it is about self-worth, knowing our true value and recognizing how many gifts we already possess. A vision of financial comfort will look different for each of us. Paying attention to the many blessings that are already a part of your daily life is a wonderful place to start.

Overspending is often an attempt to fill an emotionally empty hole. Wouldn't it be great to fill that hole with something that will work toward your dream? The work you will do to transform your relationship with money is not about deprivation; it's about creating conscious financial intention!

Write It: What are your true beliefs about money and finances, and where are the roots of these beliefs? Are there any financial habits you feel ready to transform (overspending, not balancing your checkbook)? What would it take for you to transform this limiting belief?

Live It: If finances are your weak link, it's time to Dance Your Fear! (see page 118) and take conscious action. It is not as hard as you might imagine.

Step One: Purchase an inexpensive software program (like Quicken) to help you do the math. This is worth every penny and is the best investment you can make in your business.

Step Two: Pick one day a week to be your Abundance Day! This is a day for getting your business and life in order so the flow can find you, and making certain you're prepared to manage it when it does! If, after a few months, you notice this aspect of your life remains a challenge, find a way to hire a bookkeeper—numbers are their passion! The investment will pay for itself in the time and energy gained for you to focus on something more productive.

Limiting Beliefs

Have you ever asked yourself why it is easier to worry than to put that same amount of energy into thinking everything will be just fine? Creating intention to shift your thinking is an hourly practice and constant shift of attention and focus. It's time to retrain your brain to practice positivity! When limiting beliefs or anxious thoughts present themselves, take some deep, quieting breaths. As you breathe, you will be able to hear the exact negative thoughts and chatter going through your mind. The noise in your head is imagined fear, an illusion that lives only in your mind. It is a projected fantasy of something that has not yet occurred.

Now ask yourself this, "What do I know to be true *right in this moment*?" You will arrive at the truth of your experience, as it exists *right now*. Change the channel in your mind and project the exact scenario you want to create and not the one you fear. With practice you will know exactly when to turn the channel and tune in to the station of positive possibilities!

Write It: For one day, experience how many times you choose to focus on a negative or worrisome experience. Awareness is the place we start. You might find the columns skewed to one side, but that is because most of us have been culturally conditioned to focus on the negative. Let's change history. Now, for one day track all the positive experiences you have during the day.

Create It: Create a collage in your Book of Dreams depicting your strengths. If this feels like a stretch, simply gather images that inspire confidence and a sense of empowerment.

Believe It: It's a new day! Each day is a beautiful new opportunity to work with this particular practice. The key word is practice. You might find *positivity* difficult at first—old habits die hard—but after awhile, you will notice how easily it becomes part of your daily life.

Gypsy Spirit Day

My great-grandmother, Sarah, was raised by gypsies. At least once a month, in honor of her spirit, I take an inspiration road trip—a Gypsy Spirit Day. I recommend you try one yourself every now and then!

Our culture is a population on the go; we are racing nose-to-the-sidewalk to the next meeting, soccer game or grocery run. Generally, we move so fast to get the task done, we forget to look up at the beauty around us. When you take a Gypsy Spirit Day, your only task is to be curious, look up and remember there is no rush. When you head out for your journey, always bring your adventure pack (see page 11), a journal and a camera. I pretend I am a working on an photojournalism assignment for a travel magazine.

Write It: Mark a date on your calendar to take a Gypsy Spirit Day once a month. Tell the story of your Gypsy Spirit Day in photos and words. Be aware of old buildings, people who cross your path, murals, graffiti, car parts and even discarded items lying in the gutter. A Gypsy Spirit Day will open your mind to new ideas and will replenish your creative well.

Live It: The most important aspect is to remain open-minded about seeing the world in a new way, even if you have walked the street a thousand times.

Create It: Scan the photo story in your Book of Dreams and place the photo essay from your Gypsy Spirit Day in your Milestones Passport.

Everyday Bliss

Everyday Bliss is about process, not product or outcome. Think about things you love or once loved to do that have fallen by the wayside. Try something completely out of your element, something different than what you may already do to revitalize your soul. The only rule is it must be completely enjoyable.

Each day, take twenty minutes for yourself, doing something that brings you only joy and renews your spirit. Mix it up. Try Everyday Bliss at different times of the day to see which time resonates most with you.

Here are some examples of Everyday Bliss Actions: a spontaneous painting or drawing at the beginning of your day, a quick poem, a fifteen-minute yoga workout, dancing to music, cooking from a recipe you've been saving. Or try my personal favorite, a "daydream meditation," where you let your dreams flow onto your paper, using your non-dominant hand.

Live It: Your challenge is to put yourself at the front of the line for the next thirty days. That's how long it takes to create a new habit. Many women who have taken my class tell me this single activity helped them bring a sense of balance and renewal to their days.

You can do it—a month of Everyday Bliss will allow you to develop a new habit of self-care. Once you have developed the habit, you will actually feel like something is missing if you skip a day!

Dance Your Fear

As I look back on the previous twenty years of my life, I know with complete certainty that the cummulation of experiences has led me to this exact moment. The first time I had to Dance my Fear was when I left Florida and moved to the Rocky Mountains to claim my stake and live the life of my dreams. Why was this significant? Because it was completely outside my personal comfort zone! Like Dorothy in Oz, I woke up in an unfamiliar land, miles away from where I began. I could never have known how things would turn out, but that's what risk taking is all about. We never know what the outcome will be unless we are willing *dance our fear*! Here is an important, often-forgotten fact: The "what-ifs" have two sides—what if we fail, but more important, what if we thrive?

There are two kinds of fear: real and imagined. Real fear is important and is part of our genetic makeup, put in place to keep us safe from serious harm. Truth be told, we rarely need this fight-or-flight instinct, but we spend a lot of time experiencing it in our *imagination*. It is this *imagined* fear we want to tango with because it has the capacity to keep your life very small and keep you from really living to the most full.

The next time you have somewhere you want to go, but the road looks dark and scary and fear is keeping you from taking a step, take off your shoes, turn on your favorite music and DANCE YOUR FEAR!

If you feel shy about dancing, find a quiet, private space where you can shut the door and really let yourself go, or wait until everyone has left the house for the day. You can start off slow, but let yourself go.

Create It: Create a collage to the fear you have overcome in your Book of Dreams.

Write It: How has your fear transformed?

Re-envision It: Create your new affirmation about your willingness to Dance Your Fear!

Tend Your Garden

When I garden, I often "throw out seeds." Each spring I choose a spot for a mystery garden. I randomly toss seeds over the earth and ruffle up the soil. I give the seeds water and wait to see what happens next. Maybe they'll come up, maybe they won't; the mystery is actually part of the fun!

EnVisioning our dreams is a bit like that. You might not be quite ready to make the move or take a particular leap, but it is important to throw out the seeds, knowing there may be a time when they are ready to manifest. Throw out your future seeds with intention, yet without attachment. Never lose heart, as it might even take a couple of years for those seeds to take root. When a flower comes up out of the ground—seemingly out of nowhere—we call it a volunteer. Dreams can be like that, seemingly arriving "out of nowhere" when all the elements line up perfectly.

Create It: Create an intention garden. If you have a spot in your yard, create an intention garden in which you can scatter and grow the seeds of your dreams. If you have no yard, plant a seed to your dream in a pot or container. Place it by the window and watch the progress. (For more about creating intention in the landscape, read Laura Kirk's inspirational musings on page 103.)

Gratitude

As we travel the varied roads toward living the life of our dreams, fortuitous and synchronistic events occur to show us we're traveling on the right highway. When things are going our way, it is easy to remember to feel grateful. But how do you hold on to that feeling of gratitude during more trying times? You cultivate a sense of *gratitude!*

If you lose your perspective, try heading into nature. Regain perspective with the sun on your shoulders. Notice a fern, still coiled, in a lime-green spiral, waiting to unfold, or the miracle of a deer tending her speckled doe. Gratitude is the experience of being truly alive and realizing the abundance of each moment. When you immerse yourself in nature, you are reminded that you are a small part of a much bigger picture, and you remember there have been other times when things *did* go your way.

Being of service and giving back is another wonderful way to regain a feeling of abundance. Giving of yourself to others completes the circle.

Cultivating gratitude will firmly support your inner transformation by allowing you to focus on the small positive experiences, even those as tiny as a grain of sand.

Create It: Make a sign that reads: "I am Cultivating Gratitude" and hang it on your bathroom mirror. Each day you will see a reflection of yourself underneath it and will be reminded daily to count your blessings!

Write It: You may already keep a gratitude journal, but when was the last time you took the time to write in it?

Place your gratitude journal on your pillow after you make your bed in the morning. When you are ready for bed, your journal will be waiting for you! Write three brief positive experiences you had that day. Hint: Doing this at bedtime will actually implant positive feelings while you are sleeping!

The Secret Dream

When is the last time you gave yourself permission to look at the dreams you have locked in the deepest place of your heart—the key rusted and lost? Our dreams are like fragile seeds that have germinated and pushed through the hard earth in search of light. They must be protected against the elements until they are strong and capable of standing on their own. If we expose them to the elements too soon, we may find them mowed down by a careless neighbor or uprooted by someone who decided they were *just weeds*. Therefore, be mindful of who you share your dreams with. The last thing you want is for them to be trampled to the ground by a Dream Bandit! (See Glossary, page 138.)

That said, the dream can't flow if you don't let it go! There are many fears holding us back from daring to realize our dreams: fear of being laughed at or criticized, an unconscious fear the dream will require too much work, fear of failure (or success!) and so on. The following writing exercises will start you on your way toward realizing that if you dream it, you can make it a reality—fears be silenced!

Write It: Grab your Book of Dreams and make a free association list with this prompt: "If I *could*, I would . . ." Now that you have your list, how do you feel as you read back through the words? Are the Toads doing the happy dance? Now notice what happens if you reverse the words: "If I *would*, I *could*!" Make a list beginning with these rearranged words: "If I would, I could . . ." What you should see in this new list are the small intentional steps you can take in the direction of your dream.

Leap Into the Void

Every new idea begins with a leap—a leap of faith, a leap into the void, a leap into the unknown. Is there a place you have been considering leaping in your life, but each time the thought crosses your mind, the Toads arrive? Leaping into the void isn't always as easy as it sounds; it can look pretty dark and scary. But what if just beyond what your eyes can see, there was a rainbow of color and light waiting to greet you? Sometimes we just need wings to break the fall. What if by taking small, calculated risks, you could create a firm foundation from which to jump and perhaps even *fly*?

EnVision It: Your choice, just leap: Where is it your heart wants to go?

Write It: What do you see when you look out over the ledge?

Create It: Take a photo of yourself leaping from a chair or rock. (It doesn't matter what this looks like—you're going to alter it.) Print out your photo and place the image on a page in your Book of Dreams. Alter the image by making yourself into a feisty superhero, leaping from tall buildings in a single—or baby-step—bound.

Believe It: Keep this journal page open where you can see the image every day for a week. Imagine yourself in your mind's eye taking that leap in "real time!" Take notes in your Book of Dreams during the week about how it feels to live this risk in your imagination. Remember, it is less about the outcome of this exercise and more about teaching your body and mind how to learn a new skill—risk taking!

Dare to Be Feisty

Dare to Be Feisty! Don't let the term *feisty* scare you. It isn't necessarily what it sounds like. Feeling feisty inside might be foreign to you when you first begin your transformational journey. For most of us, the practice of taking small risks strengthens this archetypal aspect of our nature.

Feisty means: authentic, powerful, bold, sassy, courageous, heroic, creative and multifaceted. Some might say outrageous, but we know better. Being a Feisty Female is all about being your authentic, unique and brilliant self. It is about wearing clothing your mother told you not to, driving with the top down, your hair blowing wildly in the wind. And when you get really feisty, speaking your truth when the rest of the room agrees on a subject and you don't! Being your authentic self takes practice and, like an actor playing a part, I recommend a few rehearsals. Find some nonthreatening ways to try on the role, and until you really feel it, fake it 'til you make it!

Create It: Create a mythical alter ego of your inner Feisty Female. You can create this piece in your Book of Dreams, on a piece of large newsprint or on a large piece of canvas pad as I did with the image for the deck. Hint: Remember, you don't have to have one ounce of drawing skills. You can cut and paste an alter ego together using images of feisty women you find in magazines.

Write It: Create a Feisty Personal Spirit Statement. Start with this sentence: "I declare that from this day forward I will . . ." Include how you intend to grow your sassy, bold and courageous spirit.

Believe It: If you are having trouble with this, create a Feisty Spirit Statement for the alter-ego you created in your collage. Give her a voice and listen to what she has to say! Ask your Dream Ally (see the Glossary, page 138) to name five feisty things she sees in you and you do the same for her.

Metamorphosis

Do you feel ready to shed an old skin that no longer fits? If you strive for growth, you will continue to shed old skins throughout your lifetime.

When you are ready to shed an old skin, the first stage of the process is to encase yourself in the ethereal cocoon, to keep the predators at bay, while you ready yourself for what is to come. The next phase is perhaps the most difficult, yet also the most symbolic. A caterpillar literally becomes a puddle of green DNA before it transforms into a butterfly. When we're in a transition, it can feel very much like that. This indeterminate period of time can be very trying and leave you feeling vulnerable, so it is important to have patience and self-compassion while you await the formation of your gossamer wings. This stage is actually the most significant, as it is readying you for flight. Now is the time to listen to your heart and not your fear. Are you are ready to let go and give your wings a chance to grow?

When you make the conscious commitment to step into the mystery, your metamorphosis begins. As you shift from what you have always known to *who you must be*, your wings take shape and, suddenly, the cocoon breaks apart and you emerge—fully formed, triumphant, ready to take flight.

EnVision It: Set your intention for the next phase of your personal transformation.

Create It: Create a collage in your Book of Dreams depicting the stage of metamorphosis you feel you are in right now. Are you weaving your cocoon? Are you emerging triumphant, yet still feeling somewhat vulnerable?

Write It: Now that you have discovered your particular stage, do some writing in your Book of Dreams about what you can do to ready yourself for what might be next.

Balance

To live a balanced life is to be in constant negotiation with the forces around us. Imbalance in our lives is generally caused by too much *reaction* and not enough *pro-action*. If we are constantly adding sand to one side of the scale, wondering why it remains so heavy, we are living reactively and not proactively.

There are two important steps to recovering a sense of balance: learning to say *no* and asking for help. Why is saying *no* so difficult for women? One theory is we live in dreaded fear that we will be disliked if we are not "nice" gals! But saying *yes* when you really want to say *no* will only lead to resentment, engaging you in the blame game.

As Rumi says, "Forget safety. Live where you fear to live. Destroy your reputation. Be NOtorious!"

Write It: Rate your *NOtorious* tolerance (the fine art of saying "no").

- **0-2** No tolerance—Not in my vocabulary.
- **2-4** Some tolerance—It takes me a few days of hives to work up the courage.
- **4-6** It depends—Depends on the situation and I still squirm.
- **6-8** Sassy—I can do it, but it continues to be a growing edge.
- **8-10** NOtorious—It's not an issue at all!

When is it easy for you to ask for help? When is it difficult?

Create It: Create your own archetype to balance—like the one on this card—and hang it on your refrigerator where you can see it every day. You might want to incorporate "Be NOtorious and Ask for Help" right into your collage.

Live It: For one day, be NOtorious! Say *no* at least three times! Ask for help at least once a week.

Rise from the Ashes

Rejection is an inevitable part of the journey while on the road to our dreams. No matter what field we are in there will come a time when our dreams and ideas are rebuffed. It's easy to take rejection personally, instead of seeing that it might be an open door to a new and better opportunity. Many of us fear rejection so much, we hesitate or refuse to take the risk at all. Allowing fear of rejection to stop you is a shadow side of risk taking, but it doesn't have to be! You can learn from the mythical Phoenix and rise from the ashes.

When you receive a rejection or a flatout *no*, take the day (or a week, if need be), and allow yourself to heal. When you're ready, dust yourself off and look for five new opportunities to get a *yes*.

Write It: What would have to shift inside you so you would not take rejection personally?

Create It: Create a healing altar to rejection. Create an altar or shrine in your office or studio. When you receive a rejection of any kind, write an affirmation and place it on your altar. Each time you pass it, it will remind you to risk that *no*, in order for you to find the *YES!*

Live It: Grab your list of new opportunities and write a letter or make some calls!

Procrastination

Have you ever noticed the closer you get to a deadline, the more adrenaline you feel rushing through your veins? This is the buzz of creativity; it's a little like that feeling you get when you've had way too much coffee. Procrastination can be a tool used to enhance our creative edge, but it has a flip side, too: the danger of missing the target date. I call this variety *procrastination as self-deception*, and it stems from a fear of failure.

I'm sure you've spent some time yourself with this type of procrastination, and if you're like me, you've become aware that waiting until the last minute to complete a project is like playing with fire. If you enjoy using procrastination as a way to feel the creative buzz, that's just fine, but know your limitations and just how willing you are to ride the wild wave of risk and unpredictability!

If this sounds more like your typical reason for putting things off, here is how you can begin recalibrating this style.

EnVision It: How might procrastination as self-deception be transformed if you were willing to believe in your talents and abilities?

Write It: How might procrastination as self-deception be impacting your ability to fully believe in your talents and attributes?

Create It: To help combat procrastination, purchase a large laminated calendar, the kind that shows all twelve months on the surface and comes with erasable markers. This calendar will help you see a full year of your life. By adding both personal and professional commitments to this large calendar you will be able to schedule your time wisely. Set a pace for upcoming projects and deadlines. To combat self-deception, place empowering affirmations on your calendar near your deadline date!

Expect the Unexpected

Dancing with the universe and trusting what comes into view is considerable work and is not for the faint of heart. For those who dare to delve into the mystery, the only thing we can expect is to *Expect the Unexpected!* It is part of what comes with a life of creating and setting intention. When creating intention in your life, remaining open to a variety of outcomes and possibilities is an important part of learning to trust the process and will help you learn to be more accepting of the outcomes.

Believe It: What would it take for you to learn to trust the process?

Write It: How can you find the balance point between expectation and letting go?

Create It: To symbolize the unknown opportunities that lie behind doors not yet opened, create a set of hinged doors in your journal. Turn to page 125 to see a tutorial.

THE UNExPECtED . . .

10 Journal Page Hinged-Door Frame

Embracing the unexpected as your new mantra, create this set of hinged doors to create an element of surprise on your Expect the Unexpected page in your Book of Dreams.

What You Need

- scissors
- metal repair tape
- image to go behind window (with white space around it)
- scribe
- gel medium
- acrylic paints: Payne's Grey, Burnt Umber and Burnt Sienna (Golden)
- scrap paper
- brush or palette knife
- paper towel
- India ink (optional)
- decorative paper
- brass fasteners, 2
- epoxy

1 Using scissors, cut three strips from a 6″ (15cm) length of metal repair tape that are about ¾″ (19mm) wide.

2 Do not trim down your photo from the sheet you printed it out on. Take one strip of tape and position it along one side of the image. Use the point of your scissors to lightly score a line marking the length of the image. Cut at that line and stick the tape along the outside edge of the image. Repeat for the other side.

3

Cut a piece of tape and apply it to the top edge of the image. Use the scribe or something similar to "draw" scrolling lines or doodles into the tape.

4

Mix equal amounts of gel medium, Burnt Umber and Burnt Sienna, but don't mix it up completely. Cover your image with a scrap of paper, then, using a brush or your finger, smear the mixture over the embossed tape. Let the paint dry until just tacky, then, using a paper towel, gently rub off some of the color, revealing the embossed lines and the tape.

5

Next, rub on a little Payne's grey or India ink, and rub off as much or as little as you like. To create doors, set a length of tape over the image so it starts at the top of the inked strip. Score a line at the bottom of the image. Also score a peak, centered over the top of the image.

6

Cut the door shape out and repeat for a second door. Peel the backing off of the doors and stick them to a piece of decorative paper. Use your fingers to smooth out all of the bubbles. Then, cut the door shapes out with scissors.

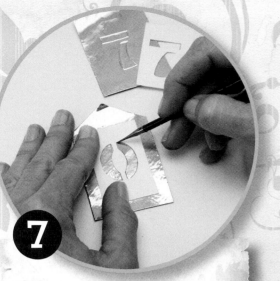

7

Emboss the doors however you like. Here, I wanted to use a zero and a seven to mark a special occasion, so I traced some stencils. I also added some birds and a few other decorative marks.

8

Score a hinge along the outside of each door, about ⅛″ (3mm) in from the edge. Fold each door along the scored lines. Run a thin bead of epoxy down the side of the frame where the hinge will go.

9

Repeat for the other door and let the glue cure completely. Cut the door piece out from the larger piece of paper, using scissors.

10

Glue the door piece into your journal. Cut the flanges off the fasteners and use epoxy to glue them to the doors as little door knobs.

⑪ Creating Your Own Transformation Deck

How would you like to create an art of intention deck that is specific to your own personal transformation, supporting the changes you desire? These steps will show you how to create one version of a card, but as you can see, there are no rules. Creating your own deck will let you bring your personality, beliefs and life experiences into your *Creative Awakenings* adventure.

As you move through the months of *Creative Awakenings*, you will notice that personal themes, stories, beliefs, myths, opportunites and mantras will be revealed. Keep a running list of these discoveries to use as the basis to create your own personal deck to use with your Book of Dreams.

What You Need

- cardstock, 11″ × 14″ (28cm × 36cm)
- cardstock, 8½″ × 11″ (22cm × 28cm)
- digital photographs
- tissue paper
- assorted decorative papers
- ephemera
- magazine clippings (for personal use only)
- glue stick
- scissors
- ink-jet printer
- acrylic paints
- brushes
- paper towels
- gel medium
- oil pastels
- colored pencils
- paint pen

1

Begin by printing out an image from your computer onto tissue paper. To do this, take a standard 8½″ × 11″ (22cm × 28cm) piece of cardstock and run a line of glue stick around just the outside. Smooth a piece of tissue over the cardstock and trim any excess tissue flush with the cardstock. Run this paper through your printer, then trim the image from the paper. Set this aside; you will come back to it. HINT: It's easier to cut the image out if you keep the backing paper behind it, even though the tissue will be independent of the cardstock.

2

Cut the 11″ × 14″ (28cm × 36cm) piece of cardstock into eighths to make eight cards for your deck.

3 Glue random scraps of paper or ephemera to your base card. Trim any excess overhang with scissors.

4 Beginning with a light color, brush a thin layer of paint over the entire surface of the card.

5 Layer a second color over the first, keeping the color more concentrated in some areas than others. Excess color can be dabbed off with a paper towel. End with the darkest color, keeping the color just around the perimeter of the card.

6 Let the paint dry thoroughly. Brush a light coat of gel medium over the card in the area where the image will go, then gently set the image over the medium.

7

Smooth the image down gently, then brush additional medium over the tissue—be careful, or the tissue will tear. Let the card dry completely again. Then you can start to embellish the card with oil pastels, which add shadow and depth. I also think they work nicely to hide the transition of the transfer to the card.

8

Add further details with colored pencils and a paint pen.

9

For the back of my personal deck, I use the same image on each card I create, like the cards that came with this book. This way, when I pull a card, I am not aware of which card I am choosing. Experiment with different techniques and complete your other seven cards.

Forming Your Own Dream Circle

In each class I teach, a Dream Circle is formed to help participants support and energize their desired intentions. As we move through the weeks together, an astounding camaraderie develops between the members, as one by one they reveal their dreams and intentions aloud and bring their projects in to share with the class. In doing so, a sacred space is created where members use the skills they have acquired to hold space for one another's intentions and dreams to manifest. When we begin the classes, participants are asked to exchange mailing addresses, phone numbers and e-mail addresses so they can connect with one another outside of, and beyond, our meetings.

Here's how you can create your own Dream Circle. Find other people in your area, or in the Creative Awakenings Discussion Salon at www.creativeawakeningscommunity.com, who are reading *Creative Awakenings* or are otherwise interested in intension setting through art. Invite them to form a Creative Awakenings Dream Circle so you can support one another's process. Rotate hosts for each meeting to allow the responsibility of management to shift from week to week. The host should attend to things such as reminder e-mails about the meeting ahead of time, keeping an eye on the clock during sharing time and supporting the group in scheduling the next meeting. Think about limiting the group initially to six people, or you may find there is not enough time for sharing and completing activities. As your group becomes more comfortable with one another, you can think about expanding.

The fun of having a Dream Circle is your group chooses how they want to use the process! Check in with your group and see how everyone feels about things such as a location for your meetings. Do you want to have a creative and fun night out or do you want your group to be in a quiet place, like someone's home?

I want to take a moment and talk about one important issue in group dynamics—building trust. Bringing people together, some who may already know one another and others who may not, requires some skill, but you can easily build trust in your group by creating sacred structure.

Confidentiality

Create a sacred agreement about keeping things within the group. It is worth spending some time on this, as it will be the thread that binds your group together. You'll want to talk about what this means to each of you in your group. For each group and each member, it will be different. Allow each person to identify his or her personal needs around confidentiality. For example, "I feel that whatever is discussed in this group remains in this group. If you want to talk about *your* personal experiences with others, that is fine, but please keep my stories, sacred to the circle." Once you have agreed on how this will look for your particular group, *honor this commitment.* You can even write something up, hand it out at the second meeting and place it in your Book of Dreams. It will empower your group as you move through life's changes together, knowing there is a sacred intention in this regard.

The Dream Circle Check-in

Each person should only take about five to ten minutes to update the group with their progress, depending on the time you have alloted for your circle. The designated host will be responsible for this aspect during the meeting. A chime is a lovely way to help people stay on track and keep track of time. Here are some things you might want to have everyone share.

1. Name one challenge that came up for you this week. Share some pages from your Book of Dreams. How are they significant to you?

2. Addressing the Venomous Toad Committee. Name any negative voices you heard this week.

3. ReEnvision It (see page 110). Transform one of those voices into a new Personal Spirit Statement (see Dare to Be Feisty, page 121) that you can create during the evening on a new page.

4. Celebrate your Success: Share one page from your Milestones Passport (page 28) created since the last meeting.

5. What has been your biggest "Aha!"?

Closing the Circle

Once each person has had time to share, make a new date for your next meeting. (Get into the habit of bringing a calendar to the meeting.) This cements your commitment. Sometimes it is best to pick a certain day each month to meet, like the first Monday; this way members can plan around that specific date.

The Awakenings Round-Robin Journal

May 2008: This project was my favorite piece of the *Creative Awakenings* collaboration. When I received the completed journal, it brought tears to my eyes. It has become a symbolic representation—a woven tapestry of our lives and dreams experienced—of our twelve-month journey. Upon completion of our project, each artist received a copy of the Awakenings Journal to have as a reminder of our Dream Circle and the sacred intentions we shared.

She danced about

till the eggs were all broke

Footprints she let fly;

frisking at evening hours,

a sinewy heart

in the living Present!

She has wisdom.
To bring all this to pass,
She is the mother of art.
It is a question of vision.
We need to see.

Creating Community

The borders and boundaries of our states or nations no longer limit us from forming community all over the world! Blogs, Web sites and discussion forums give you the ability to have a creative community at the touch of your keyboard! Put on your bathing suit; let's go surfing! Start by doing an Internet search of an interest or passion. Then follow random links listed in the blogs you discover. You will be amazed at what you find. It's a creative expedition, without the price of the ticket.

If you feel shy at first, it's okay to lurk, but don't lurk for too long. We have all been newbies. Take a risk, be bold, share a thought, a journal page or a piece of art. This one activity will give you hours of creative inspiration.

We have created a way for you to get your feet wet. Join us at the interactive Creative Awakenings Discussion Salon. Here you can meet others who are

I AM ART.

using the book and the EnVision Process to form intentions in their lives. Post your projects and writings. Share your adventures. Post your projects and writings, and feel free to share new ideas you might discover along the road to your Creative Awakening.

www.creativeawakeningscommunity.com

MILE MARKER 12 Creating Your Own Round-Robin Journal

Hosting your own Awakenings Round-Robin is simple and fun. The Awakenings Journal is a creative way to stay connected with other participants and also hold space for one another's dreams and intentions to manifest. Use the deck to support you in creating the pages for the journal, and don't forget to add an Exquisite Corpse to the process (see Glossary, page 138). Here's how to get started!

What You Need

small 3″ × 5″ (8cm × 13cm) blank journal

mixed-media collage supplies

small bulldog clip

1

Select the participants of your round-robin.

2

There are two ways you can play: a) One person creates a single journal and that journal is rotated around to all the players. You end up with only a single journal, but once completed you can make color copies to distribute to all the players. b) Each participant can create an Awakenings Journal and each one is rotated around the group. This way each player will have a journal upon completion, though it does require each member to make a contribution to each person's journal, so this is a bit larger of a commitment.

3

When it is your turn to work in a journal, open it to a new full spread (two adjoining pages). Pull a card from the transformation deck.

4

Create a mini-collage on the spread, leaving room for your Exquisite Corpse Writing. The concept here is to create a wild, surreal poem, that builds on only one revealed line at a time. The first person to work in the journal will begin the Corpse. Begin by writing a sentence on the collage you created in response to the card you pulled from the deck.

5

The first person will then send the Awakenings Journal to the next person, open to his or her full spread.

6

The second person who receives the journal will repeat Steps 3–4, working on the next blank spread in the journal, with one important change: This time when the journal is sent out, they will clip shut the first player's pages, so only their freshly created pages and writing are showing for the third player. The third player will repeat this step so players one and two are clipped shut and so on and so on.

Glossary of Terms and Sheri-isms

Archetypes 1. Jungian term meaning universal myths, symbols, rituals and instincts, influencing and informing human thought and behavior. 2. Historically related to mankind and the collective unconscious.

Appropriate 1. To adapt something into something else. 2. To alter. 3. Respect copyrights; this is suggested for personal use only.

Beginner's Mind 1. A Zen Buddhist concept simply meaning starting right where you are. . . as a beginner ready to learn. 2. Letting go of ego. 3. An attitude of openness.

Contemplative 1. Meditative, calm, thoughtful. 2. Someone who practices spiritual contemplation.

Dream Ally 1. A partner to support you in stepping into the Creative Awakenings journey. 2. A co-creative accomplice willing to cheer you on and give you a swift kick in the tushie, if you fall off the creativity wagon.

Dream Bandit 1. Someone who will trample or discount your dream.

Edge 1. The feeling of discomfort we experience, where the possibility of transformation and change lives. 2. The blurred line between ideas such as shadow/light, success/failure. 3. The edge of the void or unknown.

Ephemera 1. Simply put, stuff! 2. Papers, buttons, baubles, photos, color copies, torn pages, scraps of paper, etc.

Exquisite Corpse 1. Invented by the Surrealists in 1925. Also known as exquisite cadaver or rotating corpse. Collaborators add to the words or images in a sequence, by viewing only the word or image of the previous person creating a collaborative sequence. The game has also been played by mail. Google for more info.

Golden Shadow, The 1. The gold within the shadow, waiting to be mined; traditionally speaking, the gold is related to our higher calling.

Guided Imagery 1. A combined state of deep relaxation and active visualization, where a person is encouraged to imagine desired outcomes while in a relaxed, open state of mind.

Inherited Stories 1. Stories and beliefs passed down from generation to generation, usually fear-based, and not applicable to the present moment.

Implanted Stories 1. Stories and myths we've been told about our capabilities, by people in a position of authority.

Law of Attraction 1. The Law of Attraction takes the principle "Like Attracts Like" and applies it to conscious desire. That is, a person's thoughts (conscious and unconscious), emotions and beliefs cause a change in the physical world that attracts positive or negative experiences that correspond to the aforementioned thoughts, with or without the person taking action to attain such experiences.

Limiting Beliefs 1. Preconceived thoughts, ideas and presumptions that if left intact, will keep us from knowing our true potential. May also be related to worried mind.

Mantra 1. A poem, sound or syllable used as a spiritual conduit. 2. An affirmation or slogan created to inspire and live by.

Projection 1. A defense mechanism in which we find our own thought, feeling or emotion unacceptable, so we project (put it on to) someone else, thus bypassing what we are really feeling but aren't ready to own. 2. Largely attributed to Sigmund Freud. 3. What happens in a movie theater.

Random Revelry 1. To inspire. 2. Random acts of ingenuity, talent, vision, hope, imagination, genius.

Ritual 1. A ceremony of recognition. 2. Traditionally used to celebrate an event or let go of one.

Shadow, The 1. Jungian terminology meaning the dark and unknown aspects of our life that can also reflect aspects of an unlived life (i.e., choices we have not made) or rejected parts of our personality. 2. The dark image we see when the sun hits our back and reflects a shadow in our path. 3. The monster lurking in the closet.

Soul Session 1. A free play creative day. 2. Letting your feelings and emotions guide your creative process. 3. No planned creative objective.

Venomous Toads, The 1. Otherwise known as gremlins, the critics, judges and jury that live in your head.

Wooo Hooo! 1. An expression of enthusiasm and excitement, usually used to celebrate success.

Resources

Contributing Artists and Dreamers

Deborah Koff-Chapin
www.touchdrawing.com

Juliana Coles
www.meandpete.com

Claudine Hellmuth
www.collageartist.com

Anahata Katkin
www.anahata.typepad.com

Katie Kendrick
www.katiekendrick.com

Laura Kirk
www.laurakirk.wordpress.com

Lesley Riley
www.lesleyriley.com

Mary Beth Shaw
www.mbshaw.com

Suzanne Simanaitis
www.artitudezine.com

Amber Sparkles
www.ambersparkles.com

Susan Tuttle
www.ilkasattic.com

Linda Woods and Karen Dinino
www.journalrevolution.com

Jane and Thomas Wynn
www.wynnstudio.com

Book-Binding Supplies

Colophon Book Arts Supply, Inc
360-459-2940
www.colophonbookarts.com

John Neal Bookseller
800-369-9598
www.johnnealbooks.com

Volcano Book Arts
www.volcanoarts.biz

Wyly Community Art Center
970-927-4123
www.wylyarts.org

Cameras

Lomographic Society
www.lomography.com

Holga Toy Camera Photography Sites
www.theholga.com
www.toycamhandbook.com

Metal Embossing

Dancing Colours Studio
970-963-2965

TENseconds Studio
817-595-9333
www.tensecondsstudio.com

Software

There are hundreds of software programs; these are simply programs used by contributors of this book. I do not recommend one software company over another.

Adobe Photoshop Elements
Adobe Systems Incorporated
www.adobe.com

Intuit QuickBooks for Small Business
www.quickbooks.com

Fabric Art

Paverpol
www.paverpolusa.com

Art-Making and Inspiration

Aleene's Original Tacky Glue
Duncan Enterprises
www.duncancrafts.com

Creative Awakenings Discussion Salon
www.creativeawakeningscommunity.com

Dick Blick Art Supplies
www.dickblick.com

Ruthann Zaroff Envelope Templates
Mirkwood Designs
www.ruthannzaroff.com/
mirkwooddesigns/templates.htm

Golden Artist Colors, Inc.
www.goldenpaints.com

Movement and Dance
Gabrielle Roth
www.gabrielleroth.com

Sheri Gaynor
www.sherigaynor.com
DreamTime Guided Meditation CD-ROM

Photo Credits

Annie Oakley, Buffalo Bill Historical Center, Cody, Wyoming; Vincent Mercaldo Collection; P. 71.356.1

Unidentified Cowgirl on Horseback, Bill Historical Center, Cody, Wyoming; P. 69.1489

Vintage images in *Tend Your Garden* and *Everyday Bliss* generously donated and used with permission by:
Roger Vaughan
www.rogerco.freeserve.co.uk

Index

About Sheri

Artist, writer, dreamer and facilitator of women's dreams, Sheri Gaynor is also a licensed psychotherapist, registered Expressive Arts Therapist and professional life and creativity coach. Sheri lives in the Rocky Mountains of Colorado with her husband, Andy, and their adopted black Lab, Blue. Her company, Feisty Females™ supports women in personal and professional empowerment and creative transformation.

Propelled by passion and backed by twenty years of experience, Sheri helps women step boldly in the direction of their dreams through ongoing creative-expression workshops and retreats. She is the host of Feisty Females Radio, an inspirational podcast series where creative individuals share how they have leaped into their dreams.

Photography by Toni Grenko

Her writing has appeared nationally in publications such as *The Miami Herald*, *The Sun Sentinel* and *The Aspen Times*. Her artwork has been shown both nationally and internationally in the Palazzo Casali, Cortona, Italy. In 2002, her work entitled *Transformation* was selected by the band Matchbox Twenty and the Hard Rock Cafe for their "Signature Series." All proceeds and her time were donated to the victims and families of 9/11.

Always ready to climb the next mountain to gain a new perspective, Sheri knows she will never stop imagining and creating possibilities!

Sheri can be found on these Web sites:
www.sherigaynor.com
www.sherigaynor.typepad.com

Check out these other
North Light books for more inspiration

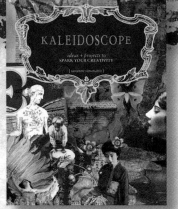

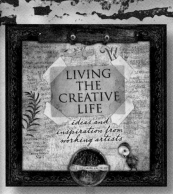

Kaleidoscope

Suzanne Simanaitis

Get up and make some art! *Kaleidoscope* delivers your creative muse directly to your workspace. Featuring interactive and energizing creativity prompts ranging from inspiring stories to personality tests, doodle exercises, purses in duct tape and a cut-and-fold shrine, this is one-stop-shopping for getting your creative juices flowing. The book showcases eye candy artwork and projects with instruction from some of the hottest collage, mixed-media and altered artists on the Zine scene today.

ISBN-10: 1-58180-879-8
ISBN-13: 978-1-58180-879-7
paperback • 144 pages • Z0346

Living the Creative Life

Ricë Freeman-Zachery

Living the Creative Life answers your questions about creativity: What is creativity anyway? Where do ideas come from? How do successful artists get started? How do you know when a piece is finished? Author Ricë Freeman-Zachery has compiled answers to these questions and more from fifteen successful artists in a variety of mediums—from assemblage to fiber arts, beading to mixed-media collage. This in-depth guide to creativity is full of ideas and insights, shedding light on what it takes to make art that you want to share with the world, and simply live a creative life.

ISBN-10: 1-58180-994-8
ISBN-13: 978-1-58180-994-7
paperback with flaps • 144 pages • Z0949

Taking Flight

Kelly Rae Roberts

In *Taking Flight*, you'll find overflowing inspiration—complete with a kindred spirit in author and mixed-media artist Kelly Rae Roberts. Join her on a fearless journey into the heart of creativity as you test your wings and learn to find the sacred in the ordinary, honor your memories, speak your truth and wrap yourself in the arms of community. Along the way you'll be inspired by step-by-step techniques, thought-provoking prompts and quotes and pages and pages of the author's endearing artwork, along with the varied works of the contributors.

ISBN-10: 1-60061-082-X
ISBN-13: 978-1-60061-082-0
paperback • 128 pages • Z1930

Exhibition 36

Susan Tuttle

Jam-packed with visual eye candy, *Exhibition 36* features a plethora of artistic techniques, tips and inspiration from thirty-six amazing contributing artists. This virtual gallery includes "guest speakers," hands-on workshops and plenty of full-color food for thought. Whether you're looking for painting tips, advice for facing your artistic fears, new tricks for creating digital art or inspiring stories of the challenges artists just like you face, you'll find something of value on every page of this amazing collection of creative food for the soul.

ISBN-10: 1-60061-104-4
ISBN-13: 978-1-60061-104-9
paperback • 160 pages • Z2065

These and other fine North Light Books are available at your local craft retailer, bookstore or online supplier, or visit our Web site at www.mycraftivity.com.

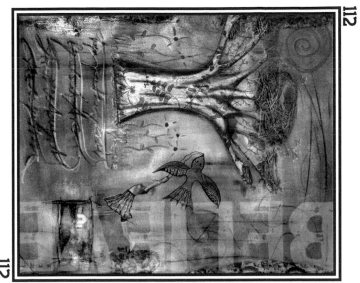

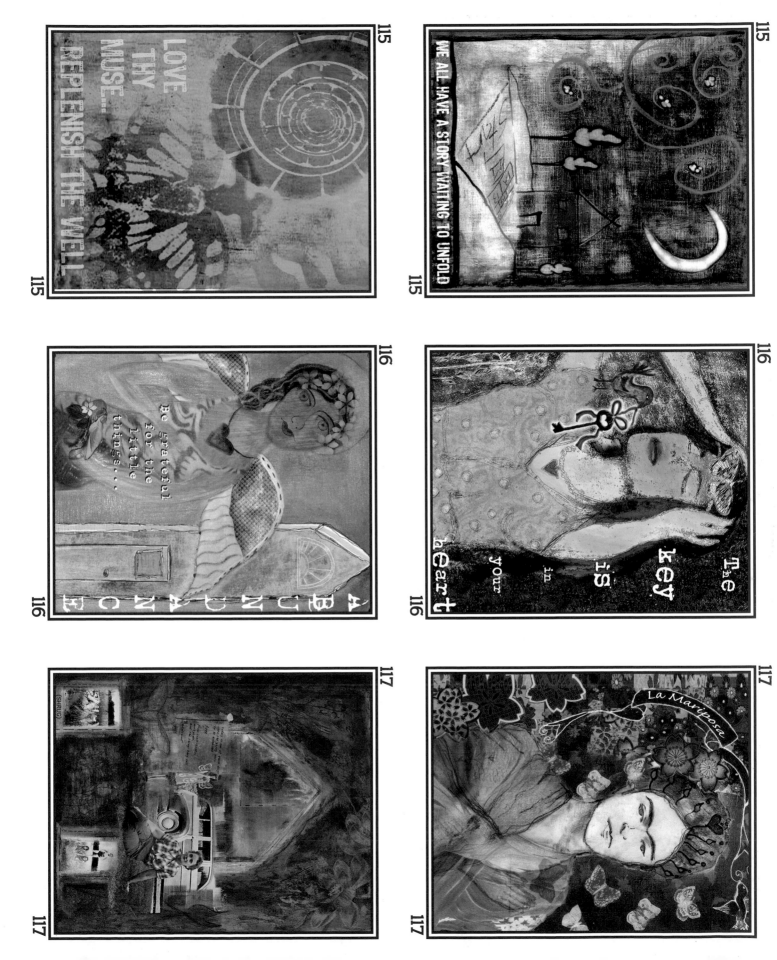

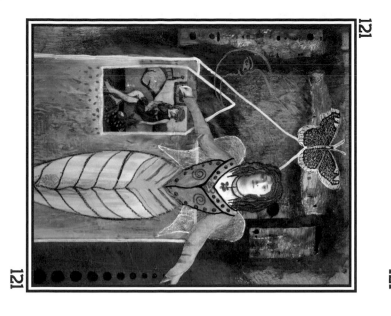

The art of balance

LOVE
adventure
career
family

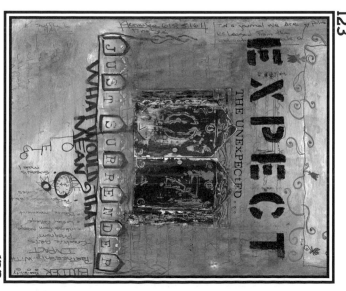

EXPECT
THE UNExPECTED...

JUST SURRENDER

WHAT WOULD THAT MEAN

TO DO